Simply Wittgenstein

Simply Wittgenstein

JAMES C. KLAGGE

SIMPLY CHARLY
NEW YORK

Contents

Praise for *Simply Wittgenstein*

"Professor Klagge gives us a bird's eye view of the philosophy of one of the greatest thinkers of the 20th century. The book intertwines an accessible interpretation of Wittgenstein's major works with the most relevant events in his life."

–Mauro Luiz Engelmann, Professor of Philosophy, Federal University of Minas Gerais (UFMG), Brazil

"There is no one more well-suited to walk us through Wittgenstein's life and work–together!–than James Klagge, who has shown before how philosophy and biography cohere. In the case of Wittgenstein, where the ideas and the life-story are unique, mesmerizing, and enigmatic, Klagge makes the philosophy not only accessible, but even relevant and applicable to current, real-life issues."

–Anat Biletzki, author of (Over)Interpreting Wittgenstein, Albert Schweitzer Professor of Philosophy, Quinnipiac University

"This brief introduction to Wittgenstein's life and work presumes no previous knowledge on the reader's part. Yet Klagge shares with the reader little-known historical gems about Wittgenstein's personal and intellectual life. Employing his extensive knowledge of Wittgenstein's correspondence and other biographical resources, Klagge shows the reader what Wittgenstein was saying and writing to his friends at crucial points while developing his two major works: *Tractatus* and *Philosophical Investigations*. Klagge's own views affect how he presents the themes in those works, of course, but even readers who have already formulated views on Wittgenstein are bound to enjoy some of the new angles and biographical anecdotes he presents. Klagge's engaging, non-combative style and skill with an extensive array of biographical resources are to thank for this little book on Wittgenstein being so accessible and readable."

–Susan G. Sterrett, Curtis D. Gridley Distinguished Professor of the History and Philosophy of Science, Wichita State University

"James C. Klagge's new book *Simply Wittgenstein* offers a concise and accessible overview of Wittgenstein's central ideas in the two major periods of his philosophical activity. Focusing on *Tractatus Logico-Philosophicus* and the posthumous *Philosophical Investigations*, Klagge explains the motivations, structures, and contents of Wittgenstein's primary texts. The compact study is simply *about* without oversimplifying Wittgenstein's intrinsically complex lifework. Klagge's study makes an excellent resource for philosophy students and other interested readers to gain competent, authoritative exposure to the essentials of Wittgenstein's thought."

–Dale Jacquette, Senior Professorial Chair in Logic and Theoretical Philosophy at the University of Bern, Switzerland

"*Simply Wittgenstein* is a lucidly concentrated presentation of the main lines of thought in Wittgenstein's two major works against the background of Wittgenstein's equally fascinating biography. Biography is no mere embellishment of philosophy here but is sparingly and sagely employed to illustrate the character and quality of Wittgenstein's mind. In effect, Klagge whets the reader's appetite for the original texts rather than merely summarizing their content. As co-editor (with Alfred Nordmann) of the most comprehensive anthologies of Wittgenstein's philosophical and personal writings in English as well as a teacher of undergraduates for some thirty years, he is superbly qualified for that task. At a number of points, he introduces examples of current dilemmas about questions like what is a presidential election? Or is the idea of God essential to religion that show the relevance of Wittgensteinian ways of thinking to contemporary conceptual conundrums. Throughout, Professor

Klagge never loses sight of the sense of silent wonder as the prerequisite of genuine philosophizing that Wittgenstein sought to awaken in his readers."

—Allan Janik, co-author of *Wittgenstein's Vienna* and Honorary Professor of Philosophy at the University of Vienna

"A *tour de force*. Not only does this accessible introduction offer a succinct, yet penetrating, understanding of the relation between Wittgenstein's earlier and later philosophy—including his evolving thoughts on the nature of language, logic, philosophy, and religion—it treats the reader to a wealth of largely unknown biographical information. Demonstrating how Wittgenstein's methodology might be brought to bear on philosophical and practical issues of concern today, James Klagge excels as philosopher, scholar and teacher to bring his subject to life. One of the few books I would recommend as a general introduction to the extraordinarily complex ideas of the greatest philosopher of the 20th Century. I learned a lot from it."

—Dr. Julia Tanney, Philosopher, former Reader in Philosophy of Mind at the University of Kent

"There are many introductions to the life and work of Ludwig Wittgenstein, but I think James Klagge has produced the very best. Taking as his premise that his reader may know nothing about Wittgenstein or, for that matter, about philosophy, Klagge gives a lucid, charming, and wholly convincing account of Wittgenstein's basic ideas, his way of thinking, his views on religion, culture, ethical behavior, and so on. He is especially good at explaining the root concepts like "language game," "form of life," and "private language." But perhaps the highlight of this book is its set of applications: that is, how do Wittgenstein's concepts and writings help us to understand the events of our time from courtroom cases to the bombing of the Twin Towers on 9/11. Wittgenstein, Klagge shows, literally helps us to live our lives: he is the philosopher par excellence of the twentieth–and now the twenty-first–centuries.

Klagge's own clarity is exemplary: he never condescends to the reader and yet makes Wittgenstein's thought wonderfully *clear.*"

–Marjorie Perloff, author of *Wittgenstein's Ladder: Poetic Language and the Strangeness of the Ordinary* and Sadie Dernham Patek Emerita Professor of Humanities at Stanford University

Other *Great Lives*

Series Editor's Foreword

S imply Charly's "Great Lives" series offers brief but authoritative introductions to the world's most influential people–scientists, artists, writers, economists, and other historical figures whose contributions have had a meaningful and enduring impact on our society.

Each book provides an illuminating look at the works, ideas, personal lives, and the legacies these individuals left behind, also shedding light on the thought processes, specific events, and experiences that led these remarkable people to their groundbreaking discoveries or other achievements. Additionally, every volume explores various challenges they had to face and overcome to make history in their respective fields, as well as the little-known character traits, quirks, strengths, and frailties, myths and controversies that sometimes surrounded these personalities.

Our authors are prominent scholars and other top experts who have dedicated their careers to exploring each facet of their subjects' work and personal lives.

Unlike many other works that are merely descriptions of the major milestones in a person's life, the "Great Lives" series goes above and beyond the standard format and content. It brings substance, depth, and clarity to the sometimes-complex lives and works of history's most powerful and influential people.

We hope that by exploring this series, readers will not only gain new knowledge and understanding of what drove these geniuses, but also find inspiration for their own lives. Isn't this what a great book is supposed to do?

Charles Carlini, Simply Charly
New York City

Acknowledgements

The approach of this book comes from teaching Wittgenstein's work for over 30 years. I am grateful to the hundreds of students who cared about Wittgenstein enough to take the classes, read his books, and test his views. While writing this book, though, I was most inspired by my young grandson Kent, for his wonder at the world and persistence in engaging with it.

Preface

Ludwig Wittgenstein (1889-1951) was born in Vienna into a family of enormous wealth and culture. Since Wittgenstein and his family spoke German, they would have pronounced "w" like a "v," "st" like "sht," and "ei" like a long "i"–Lud-vig Vit-gun-shteyen. But I have heard some German-speaking scholars pronounce the name using British pronunciation–Wit-gun-steen. So it probably does not matter very much how you pronounce it, as long as you choose one way and stick to it.

Ludwig's father, Karl Wittgenstein, was a businessman and industrialist, comparable in wealth and influence to the Krupps in Germany and Andrew Carnegie in the United States. One critic of Karl's aggressive business style remarked that "the Vienna Stock Exchange stands in fear of God, Taussig [a trade economist], Wittgenstein and nothing else in the world." The father's forceful style and influence extended to his family as well. Three of Ludwig's brothers committed suicide–two of them likely due to the unrelenting pressure and expectations of their father.

The youngest of eight children, Ludwig managed to avoid some of the pressure from his father and choose his own career, but he retained Karl's business-like purpose. He told his friend, Con Drury, in 1930: "My father was a businessman and I am a businessman: I want my philosophy to be businesslike, to get something done, to get something accomplished." In 1940, he began discussing a presentation by the philosopher Isaiah Berlin, with these words: "Let's talk business with each other. Ordinary business...." Ludwig was impatient with the abstractions and theories of other philosophers.

Karl was also a patron of the arts, receiving frequent visits from the composers Gustav Mahler and Johannes Brahms, and commissioning a wedding portrait of his daughter Gretl by Gustav Klimt. He was married to Leopoldine Kalmus, a meek and devoted woman who played piano excellently and inspired her children with a love of music. Ludwig once bragged that there were seven grand pianos in his father's house. Two of the sons aspired to careers in music, but Ludwig seems only to have mastered whistling, often performing whole movements of symphonies, either solo or with piano accompaniment. Near the end of his life, Ludwig told Drury: "It is impossible for me to say in my book one word about all that music has meant in my life. How then can I hope to be understood?"

Despite these important resemblances, Ludwig also strove to separate himself from his origins. For his university studies, he left Austria for Germany, and then eventually for England. After his father died in 1913, Ludwig took legal steps to ensure that he would inherit none of the family wealth. And for the time that remained of his mother's life, until 1926, he avoided Vienna and family as much as he could.

While Karl stood for progress in all of its cultural, economic and technological manifestations, Ludwig used as the epigraph for his second book a line from the Austrian playwright Johann Nestroy: "The trouble about progress is that it always looks much greater than it really is."

In one way, Wittgenstein did "get something done." At his death, he left behind some 20,000 pages of writings, he had lectured over a period of 17 years in some four dozen classes, he had fought in a world war, and he had designed and built a large house in Vienna. But, of those 20,000 pages, fewer than 100 were published in his lifetime. His students were few. And he fought on the losing side of a war that would largely destroy the culture in which he was raised. By all rights, he should have disappeared from history.

Yet, Wittgenstein is widely considered to be the most important philosopher of the 20th century. The popular "Leiter Reports" philosophy blog did three polls in 2009. In answer to "Who is the most important philosopher of the past 200 years?" 600 respondents voted Wittgenstein number one (LP1). He easily beat out better-known names such as John Stuart Mill, Friedrich Nietzsche, and Karl Marx, as well as other 20th-century competitors such as Martin Heidegger and Jean-Paul Sartre. In a poll selecting "The 20 'Most Important' Philosophers of the Modern Era [roughly, the last 400 years]," nearly 750 respondents voted him number four, trailing only Immanuel Kant, David Hume and René Descartes (LP2). And in a competition for "The 20 'Most Important' Philosophers of All Time," nearly 900 respondents placed Wittgenstein in 7th place. He was beaten by Plato, Aristotle and Socrates (LP3)–not bad company.

But if you know little about Wittgenstein and his work, this book is your chance to learn more.

There are three main reasons for the high regard in which Wittgenstein is held:

Firstly, he emphasized the importance of language to philosophy. This attention to language was not altogether new, but it was sustained. At first, he took the language of science to be a model, but later he came to see the value of the wide range of uses of language from everyday life. His initial orientation toward scientific language influenced a movement called "Logical Positivism," which took science as a model for philosophy. But his later appreciation of the wide range of uses of language influenced a reaction *against* Logical Positivism. It seemed that everyone could find in Wittgenstein's work something to like and something to dislike.

Secondly, he maintained that philosophy is not a set of doctrines, but a method to help avoid confusions of thought. This view set him apart from his predecessors and contemporaries. While they were trying to create a philosophy, Wittgenstein was trying to *do* philosophy. In this respect, he was like Socrates, the ancient Greek philosopher. Some philosophers might see progress in the creation of a large theoretical system of thought. Wittgenstein sought progress only in curing confusions. It's progress, but not as great as it might seem.

Lastly, he insisted on the importance of context for understanding. Philosophers may have the popular reputation of navel-gazing, as though we might figure out something just by thinking about it, and it alone, hard enough. But Wittgenstein took a wider view. To him, words were part of sentences, sentences part of language, and languages part of communities. One of Wittgenstein's students recalled that "it didn't matter what subject matter Wittgenstein discussed. What was important was the method he brought to bear on the subject, which was always the same. He always emphasized the importance of the context for understanding things—when we ignore the context, what remains is flawed" (PPO, p. 356).

Wittgenstein's writings create a certain fascination among readers or would-be readers. The one book that he published in his lifetime, the *Tractatus Logico-Philosophicus* (TLP), was cryptic, oracular, and obscure; thus, it seems profound even if it is not understood. A second book, the *Philosophical Investigations* (PI), which was published shortly after his death, was more extensive and wide-ranging, but without a clear point. It could be, and was, put to a wide range of uses, both inside philosophy and outside. Figures as diverse as Stanley Hauerwas in theology, Marjorie Perloff in literary criticism, Steve Reich in music composition, and the conceptual artist Joseph Kosuth, have drawn on Wittgenstein's work for guidance or inspiration.

But as important as Wittgenstein is taken to be, I have not met a person who has tried to read either of his two great books and come away without a feeling of deep frustration. This is especially true of readers with little background in philosophy, but it is even true of those with a good deal of background and experience in philosophy. Invariably, the problem is that the context is missing.

It is most common to put the book down after several pages and wonder what Wittgenstein could be talking about. Unfortunately, he gives us almost no guidance, and it is difficult to guess for ourselves. So, it is best to read the books in the company of a guide. That is the purpose of *Simply Wittgenstein*. Once you get to know him and get a sense of what he is talking about and why, once you see how his comments raise or contribute to issues of larger interest, you will agree that reading Wittgenstein is well worth the effort.

So far we have learned something of the household in which

Ludwig grew up. From here we will pick up the story of his life along the way, as it becomes relevant and provides the context for understanding his writings. But it is the writings–his two great books–that made Wittgenstein famous. So they will be our focus.

James C. Klagge
Blacksburg, Virginia

1. The *Tractatus*

Despite its long title, the *Tractatus Logico-Philosophicus* is a short book. In fact, it was originally published in German in 1921 as a 67-page-long article entitled "Logisch-Philosophische Abhandlung," which means a treatise or essay on logical philosophy, or philosophy done in a logical way. Wittgenstein wrote it while he was a soldier in the First World War, and completed it in 1918. It took a few years to find a publisher, and no wonder: This work is a series of 526 decimally-numbered passages, each ranging from a single sentence to several paragraphs, running from 1 to 7, with an eight-paragraph long preface. For the most part, the language is simple and straightforward, though there are a number of logical and mathematical symbols used towards the end.

The book's seven main propositions are as follows:

1. The world is all that is the case.
2. What is the case—a fact—is the existence of states of affairs.
3. A logical picture of facts is a thought.
4. A thought is a proposition with sense.
5. A proposition is a truth-function of elementary propositions. (An elementary proposition is a truth-function of itself.)
6. The general form of a truth-function is $[\bar{p}, \bar{\xi}, N(\bar{\xi})]$. This is the general form of a proposition.
7. What we cannot speak about we must pass over in silence.

The other 519 passages are arranged decimally as commentaries on the above points. Yet, one of Wittgenstein's mentors, the German logician Gottlob Frege (1848-1925), told him: "I find it difficult to understand. You place your propositions one after the other mostly without giving reasons for them, or without giving enough detailed reasons." Based on this assessment, we should not expect the *Tractatus* to be easy going.

Its publication as a book, in 1922, included an English translation and a new title. The Latin title has roughly the same meaning as the German one, but gives the work a lofty, quasi-biblical tone. Wittgenstein took the decimal numbering of the passages to be quite important, but the reader needn't take it too seriously, apart from the general sense of organization it provides.

The World

The *Tractatus* opens with a sort of cosmic creation story: "The world is everything that is the case" (TLP 1). Philosophers like to ask big questions—like, what is the world made up of? And then offer a theory. René Descartes thought the world was made up of minds and bodies. Minds included God and human minds; bodies comprised human bodies and everything else made of matter. Bishop George Berkeley thought the world was made up only of minds—human minds and the mind of God. What we think of as physical objects were just a bunch of mental experiences or possibilities for experiences. Aristotle thought the world was made up of substances, and living beings were the best examples of substances. Another Greek philosopher, Democritus, believed the world was made up of only physical atoms and void—empty space. Mind was just a complicated arrangement of physical atoms. And Plato thought so little of the physical world that he believed the abstract realm of the Forms was what mattered most. In each case, the answer to the big question was one or two kinds of *thing*.

But Wittgenstein saw it differently: "The world is the totality of facts, not of things" (TLP 1.1). He wasn't so much interested in *what* the basic things were, but in *how* they were. To him, the fundamental nature of the world was structural: Facts have a structure and are arrangements of things. Things do not exist except in arrangements.

To understand Wittgenstein's thinking, let's go back for a moment to his days as a student. Before getting interested in philosophy,

Wittgenstein had trained, from 1906 to 1908, as an engineer at a renowned technical college near Berlin. His father would have liked him to study business, but this course was practical enough to prove acceptable. Then, from 1908 to 1911, the period that coincided with the beginnings of engine-powered flights, Wittgenstein studied aeronautical engineering at the University of Manchester in England. In November of 1910, he submitted a patent application for "Improvements in Propellers Applicable for Aerial Machines." The patent was granted in August of the next year.

The patent application made no mention of what the propeller would be made of; it only explained how it would be structured. Engineers are interested in structures and models that can abstract away from the specific material that makes up a system.

Engineering work sparked Wittgenstein's interest in mathematics, and then in the foundations of mathematics, or logic. After asking around, he determined that the best place to study his newfound interest in logic was with Bertrand Russell (1872-1970) at the University of Cambridge, in England. So he went there in October of 1911 and sought out Russell.

Russell wrote to a friend on that day: "an unknown German appeared, speaking very little English, but refusing to speak German. He turned out to be a man who had learned engineering at Charlottenburg, but during his course had acquired, by himself, a passion for the philosophy of mathematics & he has now come to Cambridge on purpose to hear me" (DG, pp. 38-39).

It was Wittgenstein's work with Russell that got him thinking about the nature of the world. In fact, Russell's interests in many ways became Wittgenstein's too, as it often happens in a teacher-student relationship. Russell called his own theory "logical atomism," and that was an apt name for the view Wittgenstein propounded as well. Scientists see the physical world as built up out of arrangements of physical atoms. In parallel, Russell and Wittgenstein saw the world in general as constructed out of arrangements of logical atoms, or basic facts. We can see

Wittgenstein as asking the question: "How might the world be engineered out of basic facts?"

Analysis

Let's begin by thinking about a fact that is familiar to us—*Obama won the US Presidential election in 2008*. This may come across as a simple fact, but it is immediately clear that it is not. It is not even as simple as that he received the most votes in the 2008 US Presidential election. That is because the US Presidential election is determined by an Electoral College election, which, in turn, is determined by the popular votes in each state. So the Presidential electoral victory amounts to a set of electoral outcomes in each state and a set of rules for the Electoral College. Therefore, we might say that the familiar fact, which can be analyzed or broken down into more basic facts, is really a complex structure of other facts. Wittgenstein thought this held generally: "Every statement about complexes can be resolved into a statement about their constituents and into the propositions that describe the complexes completely" (TLP 2.0201).

It is plausible to suppose that many of the kinds of facts we are familiar with are actually complex in this sense. Take, for instance, this sentence: "John is a bachelor." This implies that John is a male, of marrying age, who is currently not married. Another example: "The cat is on the mat," could also be further analyzed. We might analyze what it is to be a cat or a mat. We might even analyze what it is to be "on" something, though that seems pretty basic.

Where does such analysis lead? Some might think this is a hopeless process, that most things cannot be analyzed in this way. Others may believe this is an endless exercise. Numbers, for example, seem endlessly divisible. Between these two extremes, Wittgenstein and Russell thought that the process would lead to a single and complete analysis, breaking facts down into their most basic constituents: "A proposition has one and only one complete analysis" (TLP 3.25). Wittgenstein called facts at this most basic level–the endpoint of a complete analysis–"atomic facts" or "states of affairs."

Russell had his own view about *what* the basic things were that got structured into facts at the basic level of analysis. He thought they were tiny bits of experience–what philosophers call "sense data." Russell was, around the time Wittgenstein studied with him, an "idealist" (meaning, in this context, that to him everything was made up out of *ideas* or experiences). But Wittgenstein did not seem interested in answering the question of *what* the things were. He just called them "objects": "Objects are simple" (TLP 2.02); "Objects make up the substance of the world" (TLP 2.021).

Many years later, a friend asked Wittgenstein whether, when he wrote the *Tractatus*, he had ever decided on anything as an example of a "simple object." His reply was that his thought at that time had been that he was a *logician* and, as such, it was not his business to try to decide "whether this thing or that was a simple thing or a complex thing" (MM, p. 70).

While Wittgenstein did not conjecture about what the objects might turn out to be, his commitment to the existence of such objects constituted a sort of conceptual scheme: Any world, real or imagined, is object-ual, or object-based (TLP 2.022, 2.023). The differences between possible worlds are just differences in the arrangement of basic objects (TLP 2.0271). Objects are the metaphysical building blocks of any world, and any world can be engineered out of them.

Language

Wittgenstein took it for granted that we talk about the world. We can be right or wrong when we say, for example, "The cat is on the mat." If a sentence can be an accurate description of the world, then there must be some explanation of *how* that can be. What is it about a sentence that accounts for its being *about* the world, and what is it about a true sentence that accounts for its being an *accurate* portrayal of the world? Wittgenstein focused on the fact that a sentence has structure, just as the part of the world that the sentence is about has structure too. He assumed that this parallelism of structure–mathematicians call it "isomorphism"–accounted for the ability of language to be about, and to accurately portray, facts in the world. This structure is what Wittgenstein called "logical form" (TLP 2.18).

When Wittgenstein introduced this concept in the *Tractatus*, he approached it as an issue, not about language specifically, but about representation more generally. He spoke of a picture and what it pictures: "A picture is a model of reality. In a picture objects have the elements of the picture corresponding to them. In a picture the elements of the picture are the representatives of the objects" (TLP 2.12-2.131). An accurate visual picture will look like reality. "The fact that the elements of the picture are related to one another in a determinate way represents that things are related to one another in the same way" (TLP 2.15).

This way of looking at things came to Wittgenstein while he was stationed at the front during the First World War: "At one time I was brought to the picture theory of language through a newspaper notice which said that in Paris at a legal proceeding about a traffic accident, the accident was presented through dolls and a little bus" (WA2, p. 279). This was a three-dimensional model or picture.

But there are other kinds of representation, such as thought and language. Just as there can be an accurate picture of the cat on the mat, so too there can be a thought that the cat is on the mat, or a statement "The cat is on the mat," that is accurate, or true as well.

When Wittgenstein asserted: "A logical picture of facts is a thought" (TLP 3), I think he really meant to state the reverse: A thought is a logical picture of facts. That is, a thought, like a proposition or a model or a picture, is also representational.

In the case of a statement, there is no obvious similarity between the statement and the fact, even when the statement is true. But there will still be a similarity nevertheless—a more abstract structural similarity. "In a proposition a name is a representative of an object. The configuration of objects in a situation corresponds to the configuration of simple signs in a propositional sign" (TLP 3.22, 3.21). The representation and the fact share a logical form.

Just as Wittgenstein used "object" for whatever is reached at the deepest level of analysis of the world, so too he used "name" for what refers to an object at the deepest level of analysis of language. But a sentence cannot be just a bunch of names: "A proposition is not a blend of words.... A proposition is articulate" (TLP 3.141). The words must be structured together; they must go together in a certain way: "An elementary proposition consists of names. It is a nexus, a concatenation, of names" (TLP 4.22). And this mirrors the situation with facts. A fact is not just a collection of objects: "In a state of affairs objects fit into one another like the links of a chain" (TLP 2.03). The objects are structured together in a certain way. I think you'll agree: "The cat is on the mat" is a sentence; "cat The on mat is the" is not.

We know a good deal about the structure of language. Sentences have a grammar, which we study in school. For example, there is the subject-predicate structure: John is tall. "John" is the name or subject, and "is tall" is the predicate. This can be extended to more complex structures: John loves Mary, or The cat is on the mat. In these cases, the verbs connect two names. It is natural to speak of a "relation," or in this case "two-place relation," to describe the grammatical structure. *Giving* would be a three-place relationship: John *gives to* Mary *a* ring. Wittgenstein exhibits the structure of sentences like these logically as:

T(j) abbreviates: Tall (john), which stands for: John is tall

O(c, m) abbreviates: On(cat, mat), which stands for: The cat is on the mat, and

G(j, m, r) abbreviates: Gives to(john, mary, ring), which stands for: John gives to Mary the ring

In school, students (used to) learn how to do a grammatical diagram of a sentence. You might call what Wittgenstein offers here a "logical diagram" of a sentence. Logical diagrams show the different logical structures that sentences might have.

But this familiar subject-predicate structure is not always what it seems. The grammatical subject of "Nobody is home" would be "nobody." But in Chapter 7 of *Through the Looking Glass*, Lewis Carroll shows us the humor in supposing, as the king does, that "Nobody" is a name of something:

> "I see nobody on the road," said Alice.
> "I only wish I had such eyes," remarked the king in a fretful tone. "To be able to see Nobody! And at that distance, too! Why, it's as much as I can do to see real people, by this light."

And a bit later the king asks the messenger whom he passed on the road:

> "Nobody," said the messenger.
> "Quite right," said the king: "this young lady saw him too. So of course Nobody walks slower than you."
> "I do my best," the messenger said in a sulky tone. "I'm sure nobody walks much faster than I do!"
> "He can't do that," said the king, "or else he'd have been here first."

Cases like this led Wittgenstein, following Russell, to warn that sometimes "Language disguises thought" (TLP 4.002). He went on to liken language to clothing, "which is not designed to reveal the form of the body, but for entirely different purposes." Much as some might wish it, language does not develop with the desires of logical philosophers in mind. Sometimes the surface grammar of a sentence conceals its real structure.

So language can be an avenue to understanding the structure of reality, but it can also be a blind alley. Language must first be analyzed into its *proper* logical form. Then it can indicate the structure of reality. When language is analyzed far enough—to the basic level—it will turn out that the basic sentences are logically independent of one another: "It is a sign of a proposition's being elementary that there can be no [other] elementary proposition contradicting it" (TLP 4.211). And so, too, the atomic facts are independent of one another (TLP 1.2). How things stand over here is independent of how they stand over there.

What's More Basic?

I have just said that language can be an avenue to understanding the structure of reality. But if you remember, the *Tractatus* began by telling us that the structure of reality is made up of facts, not things (TLP 1.1), and only later got around to discussing language. Even though the book starts by characterizing the world, it seems that we only understand this characterization from a more basic understanding of the structure of language. So, in our understanding of reality, language comes first. Language has a sentential subject-predicate form, so reality must have a factual object-property form.

Understanding the structure of language is the key to understanding the structure of reality. Wittgenstein did not make this clear initially, but it became clear later when he wrote: "*The limits of my language* mean the limits of my world" (TLP 5.6). We understand reality through the conceptualization of language, not independently of it. Insofar as the basic sentences are true, they will mirror the basic facts. But we conceptualize the basic facts as we do because language has the structure it has.

This has reminded some people of the later Sapir-Whorf Hypothesis in linguistics, which claims that the structure of a language determines the way a person behaves and thinks. But

Wittgenstein, following Russell's lead, did not at this time question the fact that the language he spoke and wrote, German (or, in Russell's case, English), was not representative of the structure of all languages. Russell, however, spent a year living and lecturing in China in 1920-1921. Of this experience, mathematician John Edensor Littlewood reported that, "He [Russell] said once, after some contact with the Chinese language, that he was horrified to find that the language of *Principia Mathematica* [Russell's account of logic] was an Indo-European one" (LM, p. 130).

The contemporary linguist Noam Chomsky argued that there is a universal grammar underlying all languages. If so, that would provide support for the position that Russell and Wittgenstein took after all, but it continues to be a matter for debate.

Language and the World

When language is about the world, and so is capable of being either true or false, Wittgenstein said that it had *sense*. In such cases, the language *says* something about the world. "The cat is on the mat" says something about the world, so it has sense. If we hear such a sentence, though, we can't yet tell whether it is true or false, just like we can't tell whether a picture is accurate just by examining it—we have to compare it with the world (TLP 2.223-2.224). In the *Tractatus*, Wittgenstein did not get into the question of how we know whether a sentence is true. He was just interested in specifying what it means for it to be true—that it corresponds to the facts that make up the world. "If all true elementary propositions are given, the result is a complete description of the world" (TLP 4.26). He equated this full and accurate description of the world with "the whole of natural science" (TLP 4.11).

That seems a pretty simplistic conception of science, especially for someone like Wittgenstein, who was no stranger to science himself. For, beyond a complete and accurate description of the world, science seems to address the "why" and the "how" of the world, and not just the "what." Wittgenstein offered a fuller discussion of science in later passages (TLP 6.3-6.372).

He took these kinds of descriptive sentences to be the paradigm of how language works. Of course, many kinds of sentences look like they are descriptive, so a central challenge will be whether or how they fit this paradigmatic model. We will return to this problem shortly.

Language and Logic

Just as language can be analyzed down into its elementary sentences, so too the process can be reversed, and elementary sentences can be connected with one another to build complex sentences. Suppose that "John is angry" and "The cat is on the mat" are two elementary sentences. We can combine them in various ways, such as "John is angry AND the cat is on the mat," or "John is angry OR the cat is on the mat." The truth of these longer sentences depends on the truth of the shorter sentences, but how it does so depends on the "logical" words "and" and "or." Understanding the longer sentences does not take anything more than comprehending the shorter ones, plus understanding the logic of those words. Another logical word is "not." We can use it to form a new sentence: "John is NOT angry." Another logical phrase is "if ... then": "IF the cat is on the mat, THEN John is angry." Logical words are tools for putting elementary sentences together.

Wittgenstein represents these various logical words with symbols:

"~p" means "not p,"
"p v q" means "p or q,"
"p . q" means "p and q," and
"p ⊃ q" means "if p then q."

In 1913, a logician named Henry Sheffer figured out that all these various logical connectives, "and," "or," "not," and so forth, were unnecessary—they could all be defined in terms of "neither ... nor" (TLP 5.1311, 5.5). This made the logic complicated in one way, but simple in another, since only one logical phrase was really needed. It is sort of like deciding to drive by only going straight or making right turns. It is simple to only make right turns, but it may be complicated to use that easy maneuver to get where you want to go. Still, you can do it.

This logical connective came to be called the "Sheffer stroke," because it was represented by a vertical line (e.g., p|q):

"p|q" means "neither p nor q."

Wittgenstein liked this simplification and expanded it so that it could connect *any number* of elementary sentences, not just two. He used **N** to stand for this generalized logical negation, so that **N** (John is angry, The cat is on the mat, All men are mortal) means: "John is NOT angry, AND the cat is NOT on the mat, AND NOT all men are mortal" (TLP 5.502, 5.51). Or you can also interpret **N** as: Neither this, nor that, nor the other, nor....

Tautology

Consider this longer sentence: "John is angry OR John is NOT angry." While we may not yet know enough to tell whether John is angry—we'd need to know which John was being discussed, and when, and what it took to be angry—still, we *do* know that the longer sentence is true. For, regardless of John's state of mind, either way, it comes out true.

You might argue that if John is merely annoyed, then he's not one or the other. But asserting that John is not angry is not claiming that he's perfectly satisfied—only that his mental state does not amount to anger. So, if he's merely annoyed, then he's not angry after all—and the longer sentence *does* come out true.

The longer sentence is what we might call a truth of logic, or what Wittgenstein referred to as a "tautology" (TLP 4.46). It is not a truth about the world because it does not depend on the facts of the world. As Wittgenstein put it, it does not *say* anything about the world (TLP 4.461). As such, he said, it *lacked sense* or is *senseless*. But by calling it "senseless," Wittgenstein did not mean to be *criticizing* it. This was just his way of saying that it is *not about the world*. His point was that it has no content.

Because the longer sentence, "John is angry or John is not angry" does not in any way depend on the world, it can be represented as "p or not p." This helps to remind us that it does not really matter what p stands for—whether it be John's being angry, or the cat's being on the mat—whatever p stands for, if it is connected to its denial with "or," then the whole thing has to come out true. And if it is connected to its denial with "and"—say, "John is angry and John is not angry," "p and not p"—then it must come out false. We call that a "contradiction." What is important about statements in logic is their *structure*, not their content. In logic, in a certain sense, we don't know and don't care, what we are talking about because logic is not ultimately *about* anything. It only allows us to combine other sentences that *are* about something—namely, the world.

While basic sentences *say* something about the world, sentences of logic, such as tautologies or contradictions, say nothing about the world (TLP 6.11). Instead, they *show* their truth or falsity by their very structure.

While Wittgenstein held that names in basic sentences refer to simple objects in the world, he also insisted that logical words like "not" and "and," are *not* names, and do not refer to anything in the world: "My fundamental idea is that the 'logical constants' are not representatives" (TLP 4.0312). They are part of the structure of the sentence, sort of like punctuation, but not part of the content.

In fact, Wittgenstein's work on logic led him to invent what we call "truth tables," which show how sentences with logical constants in them depend on their parts (TLP 5.101, 6.1203). So, a longer sentence, which contains one or more logical words, is not itself a picture. It is a set of directions, using truth tables, for how to combine the basic sentences, which are pictures. You can see this point by trying to imagine how you could draw a picture of the whole sentence: It is raining OR it is NOT raining. You can't do that.

The Proposition

Just as a complex fact, such as *Obama won the US Presidential election in 2008*, can be analyzed down into an arrangement of basic facts, so too, any proposition, no matter how complex, can be analyzed down into a logical arrangement of elementary propositions. The logical arrangement will be represented by the logical relations that hold between the elementary propositions. This is what Wittgenstein meant when he asserted that: "A proposition is a truth-function of elementary propositions" (TLP 5). In this context, a "proposition" is an assertion meant to represent the world. If what looks like a proposition can't, after all, be so analyzed, then, by Wittgenstein's lights, it's not really a proposition.

Wittgenstein's use of the generalized form of the Sheffer stroke (neither...nor) then allowed him to claim that any proposition can be represented by a logical combination of elementary propositions in terms of **N**. This is what he meant when he claimed that: "The general form of a truth-function is $[\bar{p}, \bar{\xi}, N(\bar{\xi})]$. This is the general form of a proposition" (TLP 6). This symbolic formula might not seem very inspiring, but to Wittgenstein, it encapsulated the object-ual, analytical nature of reality! $\bar{p}$ refers to the set of all elementary propositions; $\bar{\xi}$ picks out some collection of those elementary propositions, and $N(\bar{\xi})$ indicates the complex proposition formed by denying all the collected propositions. According to Wittgenstein, any genuine proposition, no matter how complex, can be represented using these tools as a logically structured combination of elementary propositions. Thus, he had established what the general structure of a proposition is and, by implication, what the general form of the world is.

When Wittgenstein was working on his ideas in 1915, he set out his project this way: "My *whole* task consists in explaining the nature of the proposition. That is to say, in giving the nature of all facts, whose picture the proposition *is*. In giving the nature of all being" (NB, p. 39). TLP 6 is the completion of that task.

So that's the big picture: The world is a complex of facts that are ultimately made up of objects. Sentences describing the world have sense and are often complexes built up out of elementary sentences about those objects. Sentences whose truth does not depend on the world–tautologies and contradictions–depend instead on their logical structure and lack a sense (TLP 6.12).

2. Some Complications

The big picture of structured facts and sentences, discussed in the previous chapter, leaves a number of details to be clarified. For example, many sentences seem to make sense but do not obviously fit this model, such as sentences about morality or mathematics. How are these instances to be handled? Wittgenstein proposed two options—either demonstrate that a problematic kind of sentence does actually fit the model, or argue that the sentence in question does not make sense after all. We will see that he resorts to each of these options in various cases.

Fiction and Directions

Consider a sentence like "The white kitten had been having its face washed by the old cat for the last quarter of an hour," from the opening of *Through the Looking Glass*. What are we to make of this? It is not exactly true, as it does not seem to correspond to any fact in the world. But it is not exactly false either, since it is not *meant* to correspond to any such fact. Lewis Carroll meant it to create a world of make-believe, but we can't tell that just from hearing or reading the sentence.

In the *Tractatus*, Wittgenstein does not consider sentences that are fictional. He just assumes that descriptive-sounding sentences are meant to be about the world, and pictures are intended to represent the world.

But how do we know when a sentence is meant to be about the world? You might say that this sentence about the kitten is in a novel or a work of fiction, so it's not about the real world. Yet, the very same sentence *could have* appeared in someone's diary.

The same questions could be raised about a drawing—is it meant to be a representation of a portion of reality, or does it come from the artist's imagination? Or, for that matter, couldn't it be a sort of blueprint—a plan for what the draftsman intends to build? You can't tell which it is just by looking at the drawing alone.

While Wittgenstein did not address this problem directly, he did provide some relevant information: "A proposition is true if we use it to say that things stand in a certain way, and they do" (TLP 4.062). How would we *use* it to say things stand in a certain way? We could, for example, check the facts to see if the proposition is accurate. If we take a sentence to be fictional—say from a novel or fantasy—then we do not investigate any further. But if we take it to be part of a factual biography or documentary, then we may. And if we take the sentence to be part of the stage directions for a set, then we might go on to create the set that will make them be true.

On November 13, 1926, Wittgenstein and an architect named Paul Engelmann applied for a building permit for a house to be constructed in Vienna for Wittgenstein's sister Gretl. The application contained a site plan and a number of drawings of floors and elevations. The fact that the drawings were part of this application indicated that they were plans for something to be constructed, rather than descriptions of something already in existence. There were also conventions, such as the use of blue paper and certain drawing styles, to indicate the use to which the drawings would be put.

Gottlob Frege thought he could sort out the problem of fiction vs. reality by prefixing an assertion sign "⊢" to a proposition, so that "⊢The cat is on the mat" indicated that the proposition was meant to be a representation. Similarly, one might prefix a "directive sign," say, an exclamation mark, to indicate a sentence is to be *made* true: "!–The cat is on the mat." Then the sentence would be part of stage directions, or an order: Put the cat on the mat! However, a novel can *claim* to be a work of history, in effect placing an assertion sign in front of each of its sentences, even though this does not *make* it so.

Recall the controversy over James Frey's 2003 book, *A Million Little Pieces*, which he claimed was a memoir. In 2005, it was picked for Oprah Winfrey's Book Club and became a best-seller. Yet based on an independent investigation, Oprah later got him to admit that large parts of it were made up. Or a movie can present itself as a documentary, and yet still be fiction, as with "The Blair Witch Project."

In these sorts of difficult cases, the key is not in the nature of the proposition, or in what the proposition claims for itself, but in how we use or treat the proposition. As Wittgenstein phrased it, "What signs fail to express, their application shows" (TLP 3.262). Investigators looked into whether the events Frey described had happened—thus treating the book as history. But Frey's confession on Oprah's TV show made that sort of investigation no longer relevant.

In the case of a book, it is, presumably, up to the Library of Congress to classify it as "Fiction" (any call-number beginning with P) or "Non-fiction"—in effect, deciding whether to prefix the book with an assertion sign. In Frey's case, the book was originally classified as HV (Social Pathology, Social and Public Welfare, and Criminology) and never officially reclassified to indicate its fictional nature. Nevertheless, the Brooklyn Public Library chose to re-shelve it with Fiction.

Consider some painting hanging on the wall. Is it meant to represent a real or imaginary scene? How would you tell?

Generalizations

When describing the world, we can make specific claims, such as "Socrates is mortal," or "Kofi is smart." But sometimes we wish to make generalizations, for instance, "All men are mortal," or "All the people in this room are smart." It seems as though generalizations correspond to complex facts, so that the latter assertion would really just amount to: "Juan is smart AND Betty is smart AND Kofi is smart." If we can list all the specific cases that are covered, we can treat the generalization as a logical conjunction of all the specific cases. Even if we would have trouble coming up with all the specific cases, as in "All men are mortal," as long as we suppose that the number of specific cases is finite, we can imagine treating it in the same way.

This would seem to be the way Wittgenstein should have handled generalizations. However, in the *Tractatus* he did not. In fact, he rejected it: "I dissociate the concept *all* from truth-functions" (TLP 5.521). Still, it is not clear how he *did* wish to handle them. When he looked back on the *Tractatus* in lectures he gave a dozen years later, he said that he *had* taken the logical conjunction view, however mistakenly (PO, pp. 89-90). He noted that he had, at the time he wrote the *Tractatus*, failed to realize that the logical conjunction would amount to the generalization *only* in circumstances in which there are a finite number of cases. But it will not do so where there is an infinite number of cases, such as the Goldbach Conjecture, which states that every even integer greater than 2 can be expressed as the sum of two primes. In such a case, we can write: "4 is the sum of two primes AND 6 is the sum of two primes AND 8 is the sum of two primes AND...." But the catch is in the ellipsis (which we read as "and so on"). And even in cases like "All men are mortal," where we don't suppose there is an infinite number of men, if we mean to apply the assertion even to the future cases of those yet to be born, then we have an indefinite set, which encounters the same problem. There is no complete logical conjunction that can be equated to the generalization.

Russell had also foreseen problems with the logical conjunction view (PLA, Lecture V). Even if we could list all the cases, our work would still not be done until we had added "...and those are *all* the cases." But that is not itself an elementary proposition or a truth-function of elementary propositions, so we haven't gotten what we wanted in any case.

Generalizations that cover an indefinite number of cases, then, remain a problem for Wittgenstein in the *Tractatus*.

Showing

Semantics is the study of how language relates to the world. It is concerned with how we can talk *about* something. Wittgenstein's model for language is language that is about the world. But can't language also talk about itself? Can't language talk about how it relates to the world? Not according to Wittgenstein: "Propositions can represent the whole of reality, but they cannot represent what they must have in common with reality in order to be able to represent it—logical form" (TLP 4.12).

So too, one might hold that pictures can portray anything in reality, but they cannot portray what they must have in common with reality in order to be able to portray it. Yet, as soon as we spell this out, it seems questionable. Consider René Magritte's 1933 painting entitled "The Human Condition" (see illustration). It is a painting of a painting and the scene it depicts. Wittgenstein holds that: "A picture represents its subject from a position outside it.... A picture cannot, however, place itself outside its representational form" (TLP 2.173-2.174). While it is true that a picture cannot place itself outside its *own* representational form, it seems possible, as Magritte showed, to stand outside the representational form of *another* picture.

La condition humaine, 1933 by René Magritte, National Gallery of Art

But Wittgenstein had a point. If we are interested in the nature of representation in general, then it does not help to presuppose the operation of representation at one level to explain it at the next level. We will have only created an endless regress. Wittgenstein continued: "In order to be able to represent logical form, we should have to be able to station ourselves with propositions somewhere outside logic, that is to say outside the world" (TLP 4.12). And that we cannot do: "Propositions cannot represent logical form" (TLP 4.121).

Instead, Wittgenstein introduced a new notion—that language can *show* how it relates to the world, even if it cannot *say* so: "Propositions *show* the logical form of reality. They display it" (TLP 4.121). And: "A picture cannot depict its pictorial form: it displays it" (TLP 2.172). *Show*, *mirror*, and *display* stand in contrast to *say*, *depict*, and *represent*. A picture shows it is about a scene by resembling it. A sentence shows it is about a fact by sharing a logical form with it. Two sentences show that they are about the same object by it being named in both.

This notion of showing is also used to account for logical truths. Tautologies are not true because they correctly describe the world. Rather, they show by their structure that they are always true. Truth tables display this structure.

Wittgenstein claimed that: "What can be shown, *cannot* be said" (TLP 4.1212). While he did not put it this way, it seems plausible to hold that what can be shown is roughly what is known *a priori*, that is, prior to experience. And what is said is what must be known *a posteriori*, that is, after, or based on, experience. Thus, Wittgenstein claimed that conceptual truths cannot be treated as experiential truths.

Pseudo-propositions

According to Wittgenstein, attempts to say what can only be shown lead to nonsense. Nonsense (in German: *Unsinn*) is different from what is senseless or lacking sense (in German: *sinnlos*). Tautologies and contradictions *lack* sense. However, nonsense is created when a sentence *appears* to be saying something about the world, but it is not. By calling a sentence "nonsense," Wittgenstein meant to criticize it. Tautologies and contradictions, because of their structure, do not even appear to be about the world. They are not pictures.

Wittgenstein had no problem with sentences like "There are dogs" or even "There are unicorns." While the latter is false, it is still attempting to describe the world. But he had problems with the sentence, "There are objects" (TLP 4.1272). Here we are not so much describing the world as characterizing our conceptual scheme. The structure of the sentence gives it the same appearance as the previous two sentences, so it appears to be saying something about the world–true or false. The problem, according to Wittgenstein, is that it employs a "formal concept" (TLP 4.126), rather than a proper descriptive concept, which, like "blue," is part of a genuine proposition that tells us something about the world. A formal concept gets at the form of our conceptual scheme; it is used to try to *say* something about our conceptual scheme, and so it produces only a pseudo-proposition.

However, assertions involving formal concepts, like "object," "property," and "fact," can be expressed indirectly instead. Sentences such as "There are dogs," and "Fido is a dog" *show* that there are objects, since names are part of our language and names pick out objects (4.126). "Greenness is a property" is nonsense, but the sentence "Grass is green," *shows* that greenness is a property because "is green" functions as a predicate in this and other sentences. Our conceptual scheme is *shown* by what we say and by how we describe the world. But we can't *describe* our conceptual scheme.

Philosophy

Wittgenstein thought that philosophy largely consists of pseudo-propositions that appear to make descriptive claims about the world, but do not: "Most of the propositions and questions to be found in philosophical works are not false but nonsensical.

Consequently, we cannot give any answer to questions of this kind, but can only point out that they are nonsensical. Most of the propositions and questions of philosophers arise from our failure to understand the logic of our language" (TLP 4.003 and Preface). The few examples that Wittgenstein gave do not seem especially helpful, such as "whether the good is more or less identical than the beautiful."

But we could consider a question like: "What is the meaning of life?" Certainly this does *not* ask us a question about the world, like: "What is the meaning of that smoke?" "Smoke means fire—we better call 911!" But it looks like it does. So it is a pseudo-question.

Wittgenstein went on to say: "All of philosophy is a critique of language" (TLP 4.0031). It might seem that "meaning" (as in "meaning of life") names some single *thing* or *activity* that we should try to discover: What is it? This contributes to the feeling that there is some secret to the meaning of life. And it may seem very mysterious and frustrating if we are unable to discover such meaning. But, in this particular context, "meaning" does not name a particular thing or activity. Our language misleads us into looking for some secret *thing* which life means.

Once we realize that "meaning" is not functioning here as a name of some*thing*, we can consider other possibilities. Perhaps what we really want to know is: "What things or activities make life *meaningful?*" This seems much more answerable, if not quite so mysterious and profound. In a sense, we have offered a critique of language by noting that what appeared to be a name, really functions as an adjective.

This illustrates Wittgenstein's comment on the nature of philosophy: "Philosophy is not a body of doctrine but an activity...Philosophy does not result in 'philosophical propositions', but rather in the clarification of propositions" (TLP 4.112). It is *not*, then, the job of the philosopher to figure out what makes life meaningful—any person can reflect on that. Perhaps enjoyment and a sense of accomplishment are important components of a meaningful life. But, it *is* the job of philosophy to keep us from asking the wrong question, "What is the meaning of life?" which would lead us astray. "The correct method in philosophy would really be the following: to say nothing except what can be said...and then, whenever someone else wanted to say something metaphysical, to demonstrate to him that he had failed to give meaning to certain signs in his proposition." That is just what we have done with the question "What is the meaning of life?" Wittgenstein continued: "Although it would not be satisfying to the other person—he would not have the feeling we were teaching him philosophy—this method would be the only strictly correct one" (TLP 6.53).

I leave it to the reader to decide if this is how a philosopher should proceed.

3. The Great War

Between 1911 and 1913, Wittgenstein studied with Russell, working on a set of philosophical problems formulated largely by Russell. These were the problems that comprised the *Tractatus* as we have discussed it so far.

In September of 1913, Wittgenstein spent a month visiting Norway with a Cambridge friend, David Pinsent. Initially, the two had gotten to know one another because Pinsent served as a subject for Wittgenstein in some experiments he was doing on the psychology of rhythm. Their bond was cemented by a strong mutual interest in music. The previous year they had visited Iceland together, and now Wittgenstein invited Pinsent to accompany him on another trek; at the last minute, they decided on Norway.

Apparently, Wittgenstein liked what he found there. He called Norway "the ideal place to work in" because it provided "peace and simplicity in the highest degree." He decided he needed time away from Russell and Cambridge to reflect on his logic for himself. Pinsent recorded in his diary:

> [H]e swears he can never do his best except in exile.... The great difficulty about his particular kind of work is that—unless he absolutely settles all the foundations of logic—his work will be of little value to the world. He has settled many difficulties, but there are still others unsolved.... There is nothing between doing really great work and doing practically nothing.... So he is off to Norway in about 10 days!

By the way, Pinsent, who trained as a test pilot during WWI, was killed in a flying accident in May of 1918. Wittgenstein dedicated the *Tractatus* to his friend's memory.

Russell tried to talk Wittgenstein out of his plan to settle in Norway: "I said it would be dark, & he said he hated daylight. I said it would be lonely, & he said he prostituted his mind talking to intelligent people. I said he was mad & he said God preserve me from sanity. (God certainly will)" (DG, p. 91). So off he went to live and work in virtual isolation for nearly a year.

What we know of Wittgenstein's work in Norway is largely due to the following circumstance. When he was at Cambridge, Wittgenstein had briefly attended lectures by G. E. Moore (1873-1958), who was a University Lecturer in Moral Sciences. Though Wittgenstein did not like the lectures, he had come to like Moore and invited him to visit Norway during the Easter break to discuss philosophy. It is an indication of the high regard in which Wittgenstein was held that Moore, a prominent philosopher in his own right, accepted the invitation. While there, he took extensive notes of Wittgenstein's developing ideas, including the importance of *showing*.

After Wittgenstein's father had passed away in 1913, Wittgenstein stood to inherit a fortune. He felt an obligation to devote a portion of this windfall to charitable purposes. In the summer of 1914, he anonymously donated a sum currently equivalent to about half a million dollars to various artists, chosen by an editor whom Wittgenstein trusted. Among the 17 who benefited were three Austrians who became famous in their fields: the poet, Rainer Maria Rilke, who received roughly $100,000 in contemporary conversion; the Austrian painter, Oscar Kokoschka, who got roughly $25,000; and the architect Adolf Loos, who was the recipient of about $10,000.

When World War I broke out in August of 1914, Wittgenstein volunteered to serve in the Austro-Hungarian Army. A hernia had exempted him from the draft, but he apparently saw military service as a test of his soul. William James, a writer whom Wittgenstein greatly admired, wrote: "No matter what a man's frailties might otherwise be, if he be willing to risk death, and still more if he suffers it heroically, in the service he has chosen, the fact consecrates him forever." Wittgenstein's sister Hermine wrote that "he had the intense wish to assume some heavy burden and to perform some task other than purely intellectual work." Wittgenstein encountered some additional burdens, very different from what he had expected. In his diary, he wrote: "The men of the unit with few exceptions hate me because I am a volunteer.... And this is the one thing I still do not know how to take. There are malicious and heartless people here. It is almost impossible to find a trace of humanity in them" (GT, p. 69). But after the war, he told his nephew: "It [the war] saved my life; I don't know what I'd have done without it" (WL, pp. 211 & 204). In fact, he continued to wear his uniform and to carry a rucksack for months after he was discharged.

During the war, Wittgenstein kept a notebook, in which he continued to write about his philosophical problems, and at the same time, he kept a personal diary, where he reflected on his circumstances and inner life. As a child, he had learned to write fluently in code that reversed the alphabet. Now he again put that skill to use. He wrote his personal reflections in code to keep them from being easily read by his fellow soldiers.

For the first several months, Wittgenstein was assigned to an artillery unit but saw no action. The only event of note was his discovery of Leo Tolstoy's book, *The Gospel in Brief*. As Russell later retold the story, Wittgenstein went into a small bookshop, "which, however, seemed to contain nothing but picture postcards. However, he went inside and found that it contained just one book: Tolstoy on the Gospels. He bought it merely because there was no other. He read it and re-read it, and thenceforth had it always with him, under fire and at all times."

Wittgenstein's near obsession with this book is well documented. His fellow soldiers nicknamed him "the one with the Gospel," and he later wrote that "this book virtually kept me alive."

In late March of 1916, Wittgenstein was transferred to the front, and by June of that year, his unit came under heavy attack. He began to reflect on a wider range of issues than had preoccupied him in Cambridge and Norway, including God, fate, will, good and evil, the purpose of life and death. Wittgenstein recorded these new topics and lines of thinking in his notebook. In fact, he noted this transformation when he wrote: "Yes, my work has broadened out from the foundations of logic to the nature of the world" (NB, p. 79).

Consider three key remarks near the end of the *Tractatus*:

> The world is independent of my will. (TLP 6.373)
>
> If the good or bad exercise of the will does alter the world, it can alter only the limits of the world, not the facts.... The world of the happy man is a different one from the world of the unhappy man. (TLP 6.43)
>
> If we take eternity to mean not infinite temporal duration but timelessness, then eternal life belongs to those who live in the present.... (TLP 6.4311)

Taken in the context of the *Tractatus*, it is very hard to see why Wittgenstein made these assertions, or why he thought them plausible. But taken in the context of his experiences at the front, as recorded in the coded remarks in his diary, they make a great deal more sense.

The antecedents for these propositions in the *Tractatus* appear in the *Notebooks* beginning in July, as Wittgenstein was under attack. We know this from the coded diary, where he wrote that he was first "shot at" on April 29, 1916. A week later, he was "in constant danger of my life" (May 6, 1916). The Russian army's Brusilov Offensive began on June 4, 1916, and two days later Wittgenstein recorded: "Colossal exertions in the last month" (GT, pp. 69-74). And this mortal danger continued through the end of July. During this time, he was constantly coaching himself about how to hold up under such difficult conditions that were totally out of his control.

After he was shot at, God and death were first mentioned in the *Notebooks* (May 6 and July 5, respectively: NB, pp. 72-73). In the coded diary, he had been calling on God regularly since he entered the service, but it was apparently mortal danger that propelled these topics into the *Tractatus*.

Perhaps only in such extreme circumstances could Wittgenstein find it plausible to say that the world was independent of his will. This assertion was expressed in the *Notebooks* on July 5, 1916, preceded with: "I cannot bend the happenings of the world to my will: I am completely powerless." Then Wittgenstein went on stoically to recommend: "I can only make myself independent of the world–and so in a certain sense master it–by renouncing any influence on happenings." The remark takes life as a form of self-coaching, but then after reflection takes on a metaphysical cast–"the world is independent of my will."

Having renounced the role of the will in changing the facts of the world, Wittgenstein retained a role for the will in changing his *view* of those facts. He had earlier reflected (GT, p. 70): "In constant danger of my life.... From time to time I despair. This is the fault of a wrong view of life." Writing in the coded diary on July 29, 1916, he equated sin with "a false view of life." And on the same day in his philosophical *Notebooks*, he stated twice what would become proposition 6.43: "The world of the happy man is a different one from the world of the unhappy man." Wittgenstein encouraged himself to be happy rather than unhappy in his circumstances as they were. This was a matter of will: "A man who is happy must have no fear. Not even in the face of death" (NB, p. 74).

We know that Wittgenstein took no consolation in the notion of an afterlife: "Not only is there no guarantee of the temporal immortality of the human soul, that is to say of its eternal survival after death; but, in any case, this assumption completely fails to accomplish the purpose for which it has always been intended..." (TLP 6.4312). But he sought something similar in the present. Tolstoy offered this epigram to one of the chapters of his *Gospels in Brief*: "Therefore true life is to be lived in the present."

In the philosophical *Notebooks*, Wittgenstein tells himself (July 8, NB, p. 75): "For life in the present there is no death....If by eternity is understood not infinite temporal duration but non-temporality, then it can be said that a man lives eternally if he lives in the present." And (July 14, p. 76): "Whoever lives in the present lives without hope and fear." This self-coaching in the midst of battle then became proposition 6.4311 in the *Tractatus*: "If we take eternity to mean not infinite temporal duration but timelessness, then eternal life belongs to those who live in the present."

The report that accompanied the Silver Medal for Valor that Wittgenstein was awarded in 1917 for actions during the first days of the offensive, proved that his self-coaching was successful:

> Volunteer Wittgenstein was attached to the Observer officer during the engagements ... from 4-6 vi 16. Ignoring the heavy artillery fire on the casement and the exploding mortar bombs he observed the discharge of the mortars and located them. The Battery in fact succeeded in destroying two of the heavy-caliber mortars by direct hits, as was confirmed by prisoners taken. On the Battery Observation Post ... he observed without intermission in the drumfire, although I several times shouted to him to take cover. By this distinctive behavior he exercised a calming effect on his comrades. (WL, p. 242)

As for the fears he expressed on May 5, 1916: "Will I endure it??" he had shown that he could.

After the halt of the offensive in late 1916, Wittgenstein was withdrawn from the front and sent to train as an officer in Olmütz, Moravia. There, beginning in October of that year, he made friends with Paul Engelmann (1891-1965), a resident of the town who had been discharged from the army. It was in conversations over two months with Engelmann and three of his friends that Wittgenstein deepened his new lines of thinking and ultimately incorporated them into the *Tractatus*.

It is understandable that these sorts of issues would gain his attention under such trying circumstances, but it is not at all clear how they connected with the topics investigated while in Cambridge and Norway. "Have thought a great deal on every possible subject," he noted in his diary. "But curiously I cannot establish the connection with my mathematical modes of thought." But the very next day, July 7, 1916, he assured himself: "However the connection will be produced!" (GT, pp. 72-73). Wittgenstein was convinced, or determined, that *all* of his problems must somehow go together.

The *Tractatus* does go on to incorporate this broader range of topics. The bridge connecting the "foundations of logic" and the "nature of the world" seems to be built on the notion of *showing*. In a letter to Russell (August 19, 1919), Wittgenstein emphasized that "The main point [of the book] is the theory of what can be expressed by propositions—i.e., by language— ... and what cannot be expressed by propositions, but only shown; which, I believe, is the cardinal problem of philosophy." This is a clear step beyond his plan in 1915 when his "*whole* task" was to explain the nature of the proposition, and consequently "the nature of all being." His project was expanded by his experiences in the war.

Ethics

The sentence "Friendship is good" looks similar to the sentence "Friendship is rare." Both are subject-predicate sentences that seem to describe something by ascribing a property to it. But in this case, Wittgenstein believed that we are deceived by language. The value of something is not just another fact about it, like its frequency. "In the world everything is as it is...: in it no value exists—and if it did exist, it would have no value. If there is any value that does have value, it must lie outside the whole sphere of what happens and is the case. For all that happens and is the case is accidental" (TLP 6.41). By "accidental," Wittgenstein meant not that it was a mistake, but that it just happened to be that way and could have been otherwise. It is "accidental" how common or uncommon friendship is. Asserting that it is rare is a way of describing the world, or what is in the world. But whether friendship is *good* is not accidental. The value of something is not just another fact about it, which might have been otherwise.

So Wittgenstein maintained that "[value] lies outside the world"

(TLP 6.41). Since to him propositions described the world, "All propositions are of equal value" (TLP 6.4). Namely, of *no* value. "Propositions can express nothing that is higher." So, "it is impossible for there to be propositions of ethics" (TLP 6.42).

Since Wittgenstein said little more about ethics in the *Tractatus*, some people concluded that he did not care about ethics, or considered it a mere matter of personal preference. This is how he was understood by the scientifically-minded Logical Positivists. However, placing value outside the world was not an attempt to devalue it, but rather to protect its value. "Ethics is transcendental" (TLP 6.421). Value is not said, or stated, but it is *shown* in what is said. "There are, indeed, things that cannot be put into words. They *make themselves manifest*. They are what is mystical" (TLP 6.522).

In the course of discussing the ideas included in the *Tractatus* in 1917, his friend Engelmann sent Wittgenstein a poem that he especially liked. Wittgenstein replied: "The poem ... is really magnificent. And this is how it is: if only you do not try to utter what is unutterable then *nothing* gets lost. But the unutterable will be—unutterably—*contained* in what has been uttered!" (PE, p. 7). And later, in 1919, when Wittgenstein was trying to get his work published, he wrote to a prospective publisher: "My work consists of two parts: of the one which is here, and of everything which I have *not* written. And precisely this second part is the important one. For the Ethical is delimited from within, as it were, by my book; and I'm convinced that, *strictly* speaking, it can ONLY be delimited in this way. In brief, I think: All of that which *many* are *babbling* today, I have defined in my book by remaining silent about it" (WL, p. 288). So Wittgenstein wanted to protect ethics from babbling, not devalue it by the silent treatment. Ethics should be shown in other ways, but not talked about. Perhaps we can say that Wittgenstein was put off by people who gave mere "lip service" to ethics.

What Wittgenstein said about ethics applied in similar ways to art and religion. Those realms that have value will not be part of the contingent world; they will lie outside the world. "They are what is mystical" (TLP 6.522). Sentences with sense cannot be about them. This leads Wittgenstein to conclude the *Tractatus* with the infamous remark: "What we cannot speak about we must pass over in silence" (TLP 7).

Thus, the account of language in the first part of the *Tractatus* spells out what can be said, and at the end, what cannot be said but only shown.

The Ladder

But just before that closing proposition 7, Wittgenstein offered this comment on his book: "My propositions serve as elucidations in the following way: anyone who understands me eventually recognizes them as nonsensical [in German: *unsinnig*], when he has used them—as steps—to climb beyond them. (He must, so to speak, throw away the ladder after he has climbed it.) He must transcend these propositions, and then he will see the world aright" (TLP 6.54).

This is a rather shocking comment—that everything we have been struggling to understand is really just nonsense after all! But you can see his train of thought: He has been telling us that the only sentences with sense are those that say something about the world. Sentences cannot say something about the relationship between language and the world. Yet, that is exactly what the *Tractatus* is about. So it seems that the sentences of the *Tractatus* qualify as nonsense. They look like they are about something, but they are not.

What should we make of this? Some readers have taken Wittgenstein at his word and decided that the *Tractatus* really is just nonsense, and the lesson to be learned is that we should not engage in this kind of investigation of language and the world. According to this way of thinking, the *Tractatus* is an inside joke of sorts and those who "get it" think that Wittgenstein has been winking at them all along.

But this reaction does not seem to be what Wittgenstein himself intended. When suggestions were being offered for an English title for the book, Wittgenstein wrote to the publisher: "As for the title I think the Latin one is better ... 'Philosophic Logic' is wrong. In fact I don't know what it means! There is no such thing as philosophic logic. (Unless one says that as the whole book is nonsense the title might as well be nonsense too)" (LO, p. 20). Since he did not want a nonsense title, this suggests he did not consider the book itself to be complete nonsense either.

In addition, Wittgenstein spent a good deal of effort trying to explain the positions he took in the *Tractatus* to Russell, as well as to his friends Paul Engelmann and Frank Ramsey. Russell reported to a friend on the first of several meetings he had with Wittgenstein in The Hague shortly after the war: "He is so full of logic that I can hardly get him to talk about anything personal.... He came before I was up, and hammered on my door until I woke. Since then he has talked logic for 4 hours." Ramsey reported, when he met with Wittgenstein a few years later, that "W[ittgenstein] explains his book to me from 2-7 every day" (LO, p. 79).

So this raises the question whether there is a difference between bad nonsense (not even worth bothering with) and good nonsense (which can have some value). The image of the ladder, as well as the time Wittgenstein spent trying to explain his views to people, suggests he thought that what he offered was good nonsense, at least in its effects. But what to make of this remains a point of contention among readers of the *Tractatus*.

4. Interlude

Wittgenstein finished the manuscript for the *Tractatus* before the war was over. As soon as he could write to Russell, on March 13, 1919, he announced: "I've written a book called 'Logisch-Philosophische Abhandlung' containing all my work of the last six years. I believe I've solved our problems finally. This may sound arrogant but I can't help believing it." In the published "Preface" to the *Tractatus*, he concludes: "The *truth* of the thoughts that are here communicated seems to me to be unassailable and definitive. I therefore believe myself to have found, on all essential points, the final solution of the problems." Yet, when he corresponded with one potential publisher for the work, he "told him quite frankly that he would not make any money with the book since no one will read it, even less understand it," and he informed another potential publisher: "you won't—I really believe—get too much out of reading it. Because you won't understand it; the content will seem quite strange to you" (LF, pp. 93-94). Given this defeatist attitude, it's not surprising it took two years to find a publisher!

Wittgenstein sent a copy of the manuscript to Engelmann who, in his return letter, made fun of Wittgenstein's numbering system (DG, p. 162):

1. Dear Mr Wittgenstein, I am very pleased to hear,
2. through your family, that you are well. I
3. hope that you do not take it badly that I have
4. not written to you for so long, but I had so
5. much to write that I preferred to leave it to
6. a reunion that I hope will be soon. But I must
7. now thank you with all my heart for your
8. manuscript, a copy of which I received some time
9. ago from your sister. I think I now, on the
10. whole, understand it, at least with me you have
11. entirely fulfilled your purpose of providing

12. somebody some enjoyment through the book; I am
13. certain of the truth of your thoughts and
14. discern their meaning. Best wishes,
15. Yours sincerely, Paul Engelmann.

Wittgenstein's sister Hermine, however, was not so confident: "I have read through your essay twice.... I had to laugh at myself because I knew from the beginning that I could not understand it and yet I could not stop" (October 19, 1920).

The manuscript was finally published as a long article in German, and then a year later as a book in both German and English, finally titled the *Tractatus Logico-Philosophicus*. But, as indicated by the Preface, Wittgenstein, in essence, was now finished with philosophy—he had found the "final solution" to his problems.

The religious feelings that had helped Wittgenstein during battle remained with him for a time after the war. When he met with Russell to discuss the *Tractatus* in The Hague, Russell reported to a friend: "I found that he has become a complete mystic. He reads people like Kierkegaard and Angelus Silesius, and he seriously contemplates becoming a monk." We do not hear what he had been reading by Silesius, but in the *Cherubinic Wanderer*, a 17th Century collection of his aphorisms we find:

> Silence, Beloved, silence: if you can be completely silent, then God will show you more good than you know how to desire.
>
> If you wish to express the being of eternity, you must first abandon all discourse.

And, as Russell noted in the letter, Wittgenstein inquired about entering a monastery.

Yet, a wartime friend recalled that one night less than a year later, Wittgenstein "had the feeling that he had been called, but had refused." Ten years after that he had lost the mystical feeling, but retained the contrast between talking religion and living it. He told his friend Con Drury: "If you and I are to live religious lives, it mustn't be that we talk a lot about religion, but that our manner of life is different. It is my belief that only if you try to be helpful to other people will you in the end find your way to God." Then he added: "There is a sense in which you and I are both Christians." Still later, in 1949, Wittgenstein summed up his mixed feelings about religion: "I am not a religious man but I cannot help seeing every problem from a religious point of view."

Recall that Wittgenstein's father had passed away before the war, and Wittgenstein stood to inherit a fortune. But he had insisted that he would not keep any of this money, allocating his share to his siblings and making donations to various artists. Wittgenstein's sister Hermine reported: "A hundred times he wanted to assure himself that there was no possibility of any money still belonging to him in any shape or form. To the despair of the notary carrying out the transfer, he returned to this point again and again." The notary finally exploded: "So, you want to commit financial suicide!"

Wittgenstein knew he needed to earn a living and he decided to train as an elementary school teacher, a profession in which, as he told a fellow soldier after the war, he felt he would "come into *human* contact with the world around" him (BW, p. 51). So he set off on a path away from philosophy.

Over the next several years, Wittgenstein taught elementary school in rural Austria, briefly worked as a gardener in a monastery, and helped, along with Engelmann, design and build a house for his sister.

There is no doubt that teaching children brought Wittgenstein into human contact with the world around him. It certainly gave him a perspective very different from the one he had writing the *Tractatus*, where he had simply proclaimed his views. Russell had once complained to Wittgenstein that "he ought not to simply *state* what he thinks true, but to give arguments for it." Wittgenstein had replied that "arguments spoil its beauty" and that he would feel as if "dirtying a flower with muddy hands" (WL, p. 104). Now he had to get his hands dirty—not only in explaining what he said, but also in finding ways to interest his students and overcome their confusion.

Wittgenstein's sister Hermine recalled watching him teach: "He did not simply lecture, but tried to lead the boys to the correct solution by means of questions" (MB, p. 5). It was Wittgenstein's impatience with the students who were *not* so easily engaged that ultimately led him to abandon this career in 1926. That was when he was charged with hitting a student, and then lying about it. Wittgenstein left teaching rather than face the charges.

For the next two years, he lived in Vienna and focused, along with Engelmann, on the design and construction of a house for his sister Gretl. Engelmann was actually an architect and a student of Adolf Loos, who received a $10,000 donation from Wittgenstein after his father died. But Engelmann had so much respect for Wittgenstein that he gave him control of the details. The house is designed in a spare modernist style, both inside and out.

Wohnhaus, Haus Stonborough-Wittgenstein

Much has been written about this building, especially of the interior details: "It is free from all decoration and marked by severe exactitude in measure and proportion," wrote one scholar. "Its beauty is of the same simple and static kind that belongs to the sentences of the *Tractatus*" (MM, p. 10-11). Wittgenstein's other sister Hermine wrote: "Even though I admired the house very much,

I always knew that I neither wanted to, nor could, live in it myself. It seemed indeed to be much more a dwelling for the gods than for a small mortal like me." The house still stands in Vienna, owned by the Bulgarian Embassy and occupied by its Cultural Department.

That Wittgenstein considered this work to be the start of a new career is indicated by his new stationery, headed as: "Paul Engelmann and Ludwig Wittgenstein, Architects, Wien III, Parkgasse 18," and the fact that he had himself listed in the Vienna City directory as a professional architect (DG, p. 236).

Return to Philosophy

By bringing him to Vienna, Wittgenstein's work as an architect also brought him back into contact with intellectual friends. Actually, his time as an elementary school teacher in rural Austria had not separated him from philosophy completely. A young Cambridge mathematics and philosophy student, Frank Ramsey (1903-1930), had done the English translation of the *Tractatus*, and he sought out Wittgenstein in his rural school postings to discuss the book with him more than once.

In Vienna, by 1926, there were more philosophers who had gotten interested in the *Tractatus* and wanted to meet with Wittgenstein. They were connected with the scientifically-minded Vienna Circle, the source of the philosophical viewpoint known as Logical Positivism. Wittgenstein agreed to meet with a few of them. He soon suspected, however, that they had misunderstood the latter parts of the *Tractatus*, and he would sometimes participate in meetings only by turning his back on the audience and reciting poetry, often from the Bengali polymath Rabindranath Tagore (VC, p. 15). This was a perfect illustration of the moral of the *Tractatus*—to show what cannot be said.

In March of 1928, the Dutch mathematician L. E. J. Brouwer came to Vienna to give a pair of lectures. The Vienna Circle members planned to attend and invited Wittgenstein to accompany them. He went to the first lecture and afterward joined them for a few hours at a café. One of them recalled: "it was fascinating to behold the change that overcame Wittgenstein that evening ... he became extremely voluble and began sketching the ideas that were the beginnings of his later writings ... that evening marked the return of Wittgenstein to strong philosophical interests and activities" (DG, p. 249).

While several years earlier Wittgenstein felt he had "found, on all essential points, the final solution of [his philosophical] problems," discussions with Ramsey, and now with the Vienna Circle members, left him less certain. And, more importantly, they left him with a desire to think about philosophy again.

Return to Cambridge

Wittgenstein was ready for something else. As his sister Hermine put it: "The completion of the house probably ... marked the end of another stage in Ludwig's development, and he turned again to philosophy" (MB, p. 10). Friends of his at Cambridge were anxious to bring him back and arranged for him to have a fellowship that would support him there (remember, he had given away his fortune) and allow him to focus on philosophy again.

So he returned in January of 1929. His friend, the famous economist John Maynard Keynes, announced to his wife: "God has arrived. I met him on the 5.15 train" (DG, p. 255). Wittgenstein would talk regularly with Ramsey, and he was soon jotting down his new ideas in notebooks, as he had done during the war.

Wittgenstein had never completed a degree from his work at Cambridge before the war. Now the *Tractatus* was allowed to count as a dissertation. The viva—the examination on his dissertation—was conducted by Russell and Moore in June of that year. Before the war, Moore had acted almost like a secretary to Wittgenstein, recording his ideas for him in Norway. As Moore confessed: "I...came to feel that he was much cleverer at philosophy than I was, and not only cleverer, but also much more profound." Russell had long ago felt surpassed by Wittgenstein. After an argument about a logical issue that Russell conceded, he wrote to a friend in 1913: "Well, well—it is the younger generation knocking at the door—I must make room for him."

So as the viva commenced, Russell smiled and said, "I have never known anything so absurd in my life." It became more a chat between old friends. Russell tried to push the problem that Wittgenstein was using evidently nonsensical propositions to draw what he considered to be "unassailable" truths. But Wittgenstein was unmoved, and brought the proceedings to a close himself, clapping the examiners on the back and reassuring them: "Don't worry, I know you'll never understand it."

Moore's examiner's report about the thesis was succinct: "It is my personal opinion that Mr Wittgenstein's thesis is a work of genius; but, be that as it may, it is certainly well up to the standard required for the Cambridge degree of Doctor of Philosophy." One of his students recalled that he then, "wanted to be called Doctor Wittgenstein. He was very sensitive about things like that."

Yet, even though he submitted the *Tractatus* as his dissertation, he was already figuring out where it needed to be modified. Two points, in particular, concerned him. One was the idea that each elementary proposition was logically independent of every other. The other was the idea that generalizations could always be treated as conjunctions of elementary propositions. I already mentioned the problem about generalizations earlier. The problem with independence is this: It might seem that a simple object having a color is about the most basic fact there could be—so "This is red" would be an elementary proposition. But then "This is blue" would also be an elementary proposition, and if both propositions referred to the same object, they can't both be true, and thus they are not logically independent of each other after all. One might reply that this only shows that the proposition "This is red" is not really elementary after all. But while one could hold that position, and propose that it could be analyzed further, Wittgenstein saw that if there were simpler propositions, they were likely to run into the same problem. Another option would be to give up the idea that elementary propositions are logically independent of one another. Or even give up the idea of elementary propositions altogether.

So, Wittgenstein had some technical challenges to meet. But on larger issues, he still seemed to accept his earlier account of language with his distinction between showing and saying, and the insulation of the realm of value from the natural world. In November of 1929, he gave a talk to an undergraduate society at Cambridge about ethics, where he took the same line as at the end of the *Tractatus*, though with a good deal more elaboration. He concluded his lecture on ethics as follows:

> I ... see clearly ... not only that no description that I can think of would do to describe what I mean by absolute value, but that I would reject every significant description that anybody could possibly suggest ... on the grounds of its significance. ... I see now that these nonsensical descriptions were not nonsensical because I had not yet found the correct expressions, but that their nonsensicality was their very essence. For all I wanted to do with them was just to *go beyond* the world and that is to say beyond significant language. My whole tendency and I believe the tendency of all men who have ever tried to talk or write Ethics or Religion was to run against the boundaries of language. This running against the walls of our cage is perfectly, absolutely hopeless. Ethics so far as it springs from the desire to say something about the ultimate meaning of life, the absolute good ... can be no science. What it says does not add to our knowledge in any sense. But it is a document of a tendency in the human mind which I personally cannot help respecting deeply and I would not for my life ridicule it. (PO, p. 44)

Not only did Wittgenstein maintain this understanding of language and its limits, but he also made clear his belief in the value of what cannot be put into words. This caused his mistrust of some of the members of the Vienna Circle. Nevertheless, even while he was living in Cambridge, he visited his family in Vienna regularly over academic breaks, and on those occasions, he continued to meet and discuss various topics with some of the Vienna Circle members. He recounted the essentials of the lecture on ethics to them on his next trip home (VC, pp. 92-3).

Teaching at Cambridge

In January of 1930, Wittgenstein began teaching at Cambridge. What began as lectures on Mondays and then discussions at the end of the week, eventually became a combination of the two, with a good deal of interaction. The day before the very first class meeting, Wittgenstein's young friend Frank Ramsey died. Ramsey had worked with Wittgenstein on many of the issues raised in the *Tractatus* and had proposed some of his own solutions. It is likely that with Ramsey's passing Wittgenstein was freed to move finally beyond the framework of the *Tractatus* altogether. Instead of fixing the *Tractatus*, he could now think in terms of replacing it.

The experience of teaching and interacting with students also gave Wittgenstein a perspective different from the one he took in the *Tractatus*. Instead of pronouncing philosophical propositions, he would raise and discuss them. He became interested in why we hold the views we do—our temptations and tendencies—and what it would take to loosen their hold. No doubt his experience of teaching elementary students several years earlier had planted these seeds in him.

Wittgenstein taught some four dozen courses over the next 17 years, missing an occasional year to retreat again to Norway, or for medical work during the Second World War. During all of this time, he was hard at work on a new book, eventually entitled *Philosophical Investigations*. The processes by which he reached the views of this later book were by no means short, direct, or easily summarized.

At one stage, in 1943, when Wittgenstein felt that perhaps he was ready to have the new work published, he insisted that it be printed in a volume together with the *Tractatus*. This indicates the importance that he put on his earlier views: Even though he had left them behind, they still functioned as a sort of ladder. A colleague and friend asked Wittgenstein in 1941 whether he still held the views expressed in the *Tractatus*. He used a different metaphor this time: "No. It's like this. If you find your way out of a wood you may think that it is the only way out. Then you find another way out. But you might never have found it unless you had gone along the other way first. I should not be where I am now if I had not passed through what is expressed in the Tractatus" (PPO, p. 387).

Wittgenstein retired from teaching at Cambridge in 1947, at least partly so that he could focus on his writing. He never did complete a version that he was fully satisfied with. And when he died in 1951, he left it to some friends to see to the final form and publication of the book. His will reads, in part: "I intend and desire that Mr. Rhees, Miss Anscombe and Professor von Wright shall publish as many of my unpublished writings as they think fit...."

The *Philosophical Investigations* appeared in print posthumously in 1953.

5. The *Philosophical Investigations*

The only visual similarity between the *Tractatus* and the *Philosophical Investigations* (PI) is that both begin with the number 1. After that, the differences accumulate.

The *Investigations* is much longer, with numbered sections sometimes extending over a page or more. Concerning the brevity of the *Tractatus*, Wittgenstein remarked to a friend in 1949: "Every sentence of the *Tractatus* should be seen as the heading of a chapter, needing further exposition. My present style is quite different; I am trying to avoid that error" (CW, p. 159).

Although the *Investigations* consists of numbered sections, there are no decimals and no clear sense of organization. Wittgenstein addressed this in the Preface: "my thoughts soon grew feeble if I tried to force them along a single track against their natural inclination.–And this was, of course, connected with the very nature of the investigation. For it compels us to travel criss-cross in every direction over a wide field of thought." In one of his course lectures, he explained this by comparing himself and his job to that of a tour guide:

> In teaching you philosophy I'm like a tour guide showing you how to find your way round London. I have to take you through the city from north to south, from east to west, from Euston to the embankment and from Piccadilly to the Marble Arch. After I have taken you [on] many journeys through the city, in all sorts of directions, we shall have passed through any given street a number of times–each time traversing the street as part of a different journey. At the end of this you will know London; you will be able to find your way about like a born Londoner. (GJ, p. 143)

Even if, after reading the *Investigations*, you don't find your way about language like a native, at least you know what Wittgenstein was trying to accomplish and how he had gone about it. Familiarizing someone with a city is a very different project from laying out the steps of a proof.

For a few years in the early 1930s, Wittgenstein worked with a member of the Vienna Circle, Friedrich Waismann, to write a book on his new ideas. Waismann tried to lay out Wittgenstein's views in a well-organized fashion, explaining everything carefully as he went along. But Wittgenstein was never satisfied with the outcome—partly because his views were changing, but also because Waismann's expository format was simply not how Wittgenstein thought his views were best conveyed. This book you are reading now tries to do what Waismann failed to do, so reader beware!

The *Tractatus* consists of assertions. The *Investigations*, on the other hand, contains not just assertions but also 784 questions of which only 110 are answered, and 70 of those answers are intentionally wrong (AW, p. 235). It is not immediately obvious that many of the answers are meant to be wrong—and this is often confusing to readers.

In fact, the *Philosophical Investigations* is really a sort of dialogue. In certain ways, it is like a Socratic dialogue by Plato. Different points of view are expressed, and a final resolution of them is not always reached. The dialogue format is clear in Plato from the fact that contributions to the discussion are always ascribed to a particular character, as in a play. In Wittgenstein's work, however, there are no named "characters." Sometimes he prefaced a statement with "Suppose someone said" (PI §14), sometimes he simply included a sentence in quotation marks (PI §27) or surrounded by dashes, and sometimes he asserted a sentence without quotation marks around it, yet didn't mean to endorse it, such as: Thinking is surrounded by a nimbus (PI §97). So it is much less clear that it is a dialogue.

It is crucial for the reader to see that the *Investigations* is a tentative discussion of ideas. Wittgenstein did endorse some of these ideas, but it takes some practice to see when he did and when he did not. I think you can see the discussion as similar to what happens in a classroom, with points being made, questions being asked, and answers being commented on. But some scholars see the discussion as more of an internal conversation in which we hear different voices inside Wittgenstein's head: a voice of "temptation," a voice of "reason," and even perhaps a voice of "ironic commentary" (AL, p. 71; WP, p. 22). In any case, it is not helpful to see the *Investigations* as a presentation of Wittgenstein's beliefs at that time. Instead, imagine that he is showing us ways to think through these issues—in other words, how to do philosophy. While working on the *Investigations* Wittgenstein wrote: "One could call this book a textbook. But not a textbook in that it imparts knowledge, but in that it stimulates thought."

Finally, while the *Tractatus* is a finished work, the *Philosophical Investigations* is not. Wittgenstein was never completely satisfied with what he wrote in the *Investigations*, which is why he never published it himself; but it is not even exactly clear what material he saw as constituting the *Investigations*. What Wittgenstein thought of as the book he was working on is closest to what was published in 1953 as *Part I* of the *Philosophical Investigations*. The editors at that time also included additional material that they labeled "Part II," which comprised later on-going reflections on related material. (In the 2009 edition of the *Philosophical Investigations*, this material was labeled "Philosophy of Psychology—A Fragment.") But it is not obvious how much of "Part I" should be included. For example, Wittgenstein worked on and revised the material up through §421 more extensively than the material that follows.

Nevertheless, despite major differences between the form of these two books, and, as we will see, also in Wittgenstein's positions, there are continuities in the topics he considered to be significant. It is important to know where he began, in the *Tractatus*, to appreciate where he travels to, in the *Investigations*.

Language

Once Wittgenstein began thinking about philosophy again in 1929, it did not take long for him to realize that tinkering with the *Tractatus* would not suffice. Soon he saw the need for bigger shifts in his viewpoint. It was in thinking about language that these changes were clearest.

In November of 1929, Wittgenstein ended his lecture on ethics, by talking about "the tendency of all men who have ever tried to talk or write Ethics or Religion ... to run against the boundaries of language. This running against the walls of our cage is perfectly, absolutely hopeless." Yet, a year later, when he was meeting once again with members of the Vienna Circle and discussing religion, he said: "Running against the limits of language? Language is, after all, not a cage" (VC, p. 117).

This was a big change. What accounted for this transformation in his view of language? Here is part of the story, as told by one of Wittgenstein's friends:

> Wittgenstein and [Piero] Sraffa, a lecturer in economics at Cambridge, argued together a great deal over the ideas of the *Tractatus*. One day (they were riding, I think, on a train) when Wittgenstein was insisting that a proposition and that which it describes must have the same 'logical form', ... Sraffa made a gesture, familiar to Neapolitans as meaning something like disgust or contempt, of brushing the underneath of his chin with an outward sweep of the finger-tips of one hand. And he asked: 'What is the logical form of *that*?' Sraffa's example produced in Wittgenstein the feeling that there was an absurdity in the insistence that a proposition and what it describes must have the same 'form'. This broke the hold on him of the conception that a proposition must literally be a 'picture' of the reality it describes." (MM, pp. 57-8)

The gesture Sraffa used was akin to giving someone the finger. Sraffa's point was that a gesture could convey meaning in the way language does, and yet it does not do so by representing a state of affairs. It does not get meaning by sharing a logical form. Language does not have to be representational. Another friend said Wittgenstein's "discussions with Sraffa made him feel like a tree from which all branches had been cut" (MM, p. 15). And Wittgenstein himself testified to Sraffa's impact on his thinking in the Preface to the *Investigations*.

Even if ethical judgments, say, do not describe reality, the language in which they are expressed may serve other functions. Wasn't the account in the *Tractatus* of how language has sense correct? "Yes," he says, "but only for [a] narrowly circumscribed area, not for the whole of what" we call language (PI §3).

When Wittgenstein set out to write about his new views he began by contrasting them with a picture of language he found in St. Augustine's *Confessions* (PI §1). He told a friend that he chose to begin the *Investigations* with this passage from St. Augustine "not because he could not find the conception expressed in that quotation stated as well by other philosophers, but because the conception *must* be important if so great a mind held it" (MM, pp. 59-60). In fact, the passage has important things in common with his own view in the *Tractatus*: "The words in language name objects—sentences are combinations of such names.... Every word has a meaning. This meaning is correlated with the word. It is the object for which the word stands" (PI §1).

During the war, Wittgenstein's understanding of language had been shaped by the use of a model in a legal court to represent a traffic accident. But now he was prompted by a different comparison: "One day when Wittgenstein was passing a field where a football [in the US: soccer] game was in progress the thought first struck him that in language we play games with words" (MM, p. 55). This seems to be the origin of Wittgenstein's notion of "language games."

Language Games

In the *Tractatus*, Wittgenstein offered a picture theory of language, which accounted for the saying (or describing) and the showing uses of language. In the *Investigations*, he imagined a number of different uses of language, to begin with through scenarios where people are shopping (§1) or building (§2). Then he went on to mention the great variety of language games in this brain-stormed list:

> Giving orders, and acting on them—Describing an object by its appearance, or by its measurements—Constructing an object from a description (or drawing)—Reporting an event—Speculating about the event—Forming and testing a hypothesis—Presenting the results of an experiment in tables and diagrams—Making up a story, and reading one—Acting in a play—Singing rounds—Guessing riddles—Cracking a joke, telling one—Solving a problem in applied arithmetic—Translating from one language into another—Requesting, thanking, cursing, greeting, praying. (PI §23)

In each of these kinds of activities language is involved, but also other kinds of gestures and reactions that have meaning are used. They have meaning in the context of their use. Perhaps a good example of a language game is how people interact in a classroom setting. Depending on the kind of class—lecture, discussion, lab—certain people have a role of authority, certain gestures are used to indicate request or permission to speak, certain expectations exist as to the topics addressed and the length of time one may speak. All of these rules, roles, and expectations are part of the language game of the classroom. Describing the rules, roles and expectations, spells out the "grammar" of that language game. Such rules, roles, and expectations can differ from one language game to another, and they can change over time within a given language game. Certainly, the language games of the classroom have changed in my 33 years of college teaching.

Wittgenstein prefaced his list by asking "how many kinds of sentences are there?" and replied, "there are *countless* kinds." Three years after the *Investigations* was published, an Oxford philosopher, J. L. Austin, gave a talk on BBC radio, in which he made fun of this reply:

> Certainly there are a great many uses of language.... I think we should not despair too easily and talk, as people are apt to do, about the *infinite* uses of language. Philosophers will do this when they have listed as many, let us say, as seventeen [Wittgenstein lists eighteen]; but even if there were something like ten thousand uses of language, surely we could list them all in time. This, after all, is no larger than the number of species of beetle that entomologists have taken the pains to list. (PU, p. 234)

Austin approached language much as an entomologist classifies insects.

Wittgenstein did not any longer offer a theory of language, but a sort of overview or survey or reminder of the varieties of language (PI §122). He pretended to take himself to task for this:

> For someone might object to me: 'You make things easy for yourself! You talk about all sorts of language-games, but have nowhere said what is essential to a language-game, and so to language: what is common to all these activities, and makes them into languages or parts of language. So you let yourself off the very part of the investigation that once gave you the most headache, the part about the *general form of the proposition* and of language.' (PI §65)

Wittgenstein's former teacher, Bertrand Russell, became disenchanted with Wittgenstein's philosophy after the *Tractatus*, picking up on this very objection: "The later Wittgenstein ... seems to have grown tired of serious thinking and to have invented a doctrine which would make such an activity unnecessary" (MPD, p. 161).

Russell and Austin both assumed that a philosopher has to formulate a theory about something—that philosophy should be like science. In fact, Wittgenstein had more sympathy with that approach when he was working on the *Tractatus*. But a crucial change in his thinking came about on this very point. He came to think that there was a good deal of variety to the phenomena of life, and that attempting to reduce it to a theory—to look at it in one way only—did more harm than good. It threatened to lead us to ignore the variety by oversimplifying it so that it would fit the theory one has concocted. One should survey what there is, spelling out the various grammars, rather than try to fit it into a preordained pattern. "The problems are solved, not by coming up with new discoveries, but by assembling what we have long been familiar with" (PI §109).

Definition and Essence

A good example of solving a problem by assembling what we are familiar with comes from Wittgenstein's account of definition. It was Socrates, arguably the first real philosopher in the Western tradition, who made definitions a focus of philosophical discussion.

When people wondered about controversial issues, like "Can virtue be taught?" (i.e., nature vs. nurture) or "Does it pay to be just?" (i.e., is virtue its own reward?), Socrates realized that the issue could not be resolved unless we knew what we meant by "virtue" or "just." Oftentimes, people would spout off on these topics, but Socrates suspected that they didn't know what they were talking about. So he would switch the discussion initially from "Can virtue be taught?" to "What is virtue?" If we can't define "virtue," then we literally do not know what we are talking about. Some people might belittle this concern as "mere semantics" or "playing with words."

When former US President Bill Clinton first addressed allegations of an extramarital affair with Monica Lewinsky, he said: "there's nothing going on between us." When evidence surfaced that he had, in fact, had a relationship, he defended his statement by asserting that "It depends upon what the meaning of the word 'is' is." His point was that he was *no longer* having an affair at the time of his statement, so his statement was false only if "is" means "is and was." He, on the other hand, apparently meant "is currently." So it did indeed depend on the meaning of the word "is." This defense struck some people as a case of hair-splitting.

But there is a lot at stake with words such as "virtue" and "justice." Once we are able to define "virtue," then we can use that definition to help answer the bigger question.

Socrates' question "What is x?" (he asked about virtue, piety, courage, friendship, justice, and others) was usually met with someone's list of instances of x. Most famously, Euthyphro's reply to "What is piety?" was "What I'm doing now." Socrates explained: "I did not bid you [to] tell me one or two pious actions but that form itself that makes all pious actions pious" (EU, 6d). The "form" Socrates was looking for is what philosophers would now call an "essence" or "necessary and sufficient conditions" for the term being defined. For example, a triangle is a "closed plane figure with three straight sides." All triangles will fit that description (it is necessary), and anything that fits that description is a triangle (it is sufficient).

It is something of a challenge to come up with a satisfactory definition, or essence, for some common terms. In the Socratic dialogues, they were rarely successful. (Though, in *The Republic* Socrates came up with a definition of "justice.") However, when a dialogue ends on an unsuccessful note, it is generally because the person Socrates was conversing with had other pressing business to attend to and had to stop the search. Socrates gave the impression that if they only could stick with the dialogue longer, they would eventually succeed. He was convinced that there must be a definition.

Similarly, shouldn't we be able to define "language"? That was the project Wittgenstein undertook in the *Tractatus*. But he now saw that as a misguided project: "Instead of pointing out something common to all that we call language, I'm [now] saying that these phenomena have no one thing in common in virtue of which we use the same word for all..." (PI §65). Wittgenstein was taking the exact opposite position from Socrates. In fact, Wittgenstein said as much: "I can characterize my standpoint no better than by saying that it is the antithetical standpoint to the one occupied by Socrates in the Platonic dialogues. For if I were asked what knowledge is, I would enumerate instances of knowledge and add the words 'and similar things'. There is no shared constituent to be discovered in them since none exists" (VW, p. 33).

The example that Wittgenstein famously considered in detail was that of a game. He mentioned a few: "board-games, card-games, ball-games, athletic games, and so on." Then he asked: "What is common to them all?–Don't say: 'They must have something in common, or they would not be called "games" '–but look and see whether there is anything common to all" (PI §66). Then he proceeded to shoot down several possible definitions.

It is an interesting exercise for the reader to try to define "game." Or, better yet, choose your favorite genre of music (country, pop, hip-hop, blues, jazz). Now, define that genre–exactly what makes a song fall into that genre, or be excluded from it. Chances are you will be able to list some common characteristics and some things that distinguish it from other genres. But can you come up with a foolproof set of conditions? It's doubtful.

As for "game," the philosopher Bernard Suits took on Wittgenstein's challenge and wrote a whole book aimed at defining it. The short version of his definition is: "Playing a game is the voluntary attempt to overcome unnecessary obstacles" (SG, p. 55). That sounds pretty good. Then, he spent 10 chapters considering objections, defenses, slight modifications of his definition. Who knows what Wittgenstein would have said? I'm not sure how Wittgenstein could be so confident that "no shared constituent...exists." As far as the challenge to Wittgenstein, I would say that Wittgenstein's real point was not that game could not be defined, but that it did not need to be defined (in essentialist terms) to be a perfectly useful concept. Remember, his plea was: "Don't say: 'They must have something in common, or they would not be called "games" '."

Family Resemblance

For Wittgenstein, the unity of a concept lay not in its having some essence, but in "a complicated network of similarities overlapping and criss-crossing, similarities in the large and in the small" (PI §66). In the case of the blues genre of music, we can point to similarities of history, lyrical subject matter, chord progressions, and rhythms, but not all examples of blues will share them, and they may be shared with songs from other genres. Still, they give the best sense of what the blues is.

This variety of affinities holds its instances together in a way that is workable for most purposes. Wittgenstein said, "I can think of no better expression to characterize these similarities than 'family resemblances'; for the various resemblances between members of a family—build, features, colour of eyes, gait, temperament, and so on and so forth—overlap and criss-cross in the same way. And I shall say: 'games' form a family."

The resemblances within Wittgenstein's own family were powerful. As noted at the start of this book, his father's temperament as a businessman influenced Ludwig himself in his self-conception as a philosopher. Yet, his other brothers were more artistic and unable to accept that pressure.

Three of the brothers committed suicide—one or perhaps two because of their inability to accommodate their father's pressure. Another of Ludwig's brothers killed himself during the war because the soldiers under his command refused to obey his orders. An older brother seems to have ended his life because he could not bring himself to follow his father's "orders." Ludwig himself struggled with suicidal thoughts very consciously–especially from his mid-20s (while studying at Cambridge before the war) through his late 30s (while training to be a teacher and later as a teacher). The reasons for this inner struggle were not always clear. Russell recalled his time with Wittgenstein at Cambridge before the war:

> He used to come to me every evening at midnight, and pace up and down my room like a wild beast for three hours in agitated silence. Once I said to him: "Are you thinking about logic or about your sins?" "Both!" he replied, and continued his pacing. I did not like to suggest that it was time for bed, as it seemed probable both to him and me that on leaving me he would commit suicide.

Suicide threatened to become a kind of common thread that ran though the Wittgenstein family.

On the positive side, love of music was another family trait. While this stemmed from Ludwig's mother, it seems to have been shared by all. His brother Paul, who was a talented pianist, lost his right arm during the war. Ludwig feared for what this would mean for him: "What sort of philosophy would be needed to get over this?" (October 28, 1914, GT, p. 35). Yet, Paul had the strength to overcome this tragic setback. He went on to have a successful career as a pianist and as a piano teacher. He even commissioned piano works for the left hand from composers such as Maurice Ravel and Sergei Prokofiev. Ravel's "Piano Concerto for the Left Hand" and Paul Wittgenstein's story were the theme of an episode of the TV show "M*A*S*H" (Season 8, Episode 19: "Morale Victory").

Of course, love of music would not distinguish the Wittgensteins from all other families. Perhaps the combination of business and music is rarer. But that was not even shared by all in the family.

The suicides indicate a seriousness of purpose in the family. Wittgenstein is reported to have insisted: "Of this I am certain, that we are not here in order to have a good time" (CW, p. 88). He "saw life as a task," and often recommended, "Go the bloody hard way." All told, these characteristics do give a sense of the Wittgenstein family, and of Ludwig in particular.

In explaining the unity of a concept, Wittgenstein goes on to add another metaphor: "In the spinning of thread we twist fibre on fibre. And the strength of the thread resides not in the fact that some one fibre runs through its whole length, but in the overlapping of many fibres" (PI §67).

Socrates sought an essential definition so that he could use it to resolve his controversial issues: "Tell me then what this form itself is, so that I may look upon it and, using it as a model, say that any action of yours or another's that is of that kind is pious, or if it is not that it is not" (EU, 6e). But this supposes that there is a precision to definitions. Wittgenstein rejected the need for this precision: "We don't know the boundaries because none have been drawn. ... we can draw a boundary—for a special purpose. Does it take this to make the concept useable? Not at all!" (PI §69).

Here we see how practical Wittgenstein was. Vagueness and inexactness do not constitute problems if vague or inexact concepts serve our purposes. Socrates supposed there was some ideal of precision that all concepts must have. But Wittgenstein was interested in the varied and ordinary ways in which we use our concepts. We do not solve philosophical perplexities by discovering a precision previously unknown, but by appreciating the imprecision that suffices for our everyday purposes. If we happen to need a high degree of precision for some purpose, then we can "precisify" a concept for that purpose, but that does not tell us anything about the true nature of the concept. A "pace" may suffice to lay out the bases for a sandlot baseball game at 36 paces apart, even if we do not have a precise definition of pace. We could define a pace as 75 centimeters (PI §69), but it is doubtful that this will improve the game.

Exactness and inexactness depend on one's purposes. "Am I inexact when I do not give our distance from the sun to the nearest foot, or tell the joiner the width of a table to the nearest thousandth of an inch? No *single* ideal of exactness has been laid down ... unless you yourself lay down what is to be so called" (PI §88).

Wittgenstein's own standards for exactness, however, were far from ordinary. When he was building the house for his sister, he designed corner radiators. His sister Hermine recounted:

> Each of these corner radiators consists of two parts standing precisely at right angles to each other and with a space between them, the size of which has been calculated down to the last millimeter. ... it became clear that the kind of thing Ludwig had in mind could not be cast anywhere in Austria. Castings ... were then obtained from abroad, but at first it seemed impossible to achieve with them the degree of precision demanded by Ludwig. Whole batches of pipe sections had to be rejected as unusable, others had to be machined to an accuracy of within half a millimeter ... caus[ing] great difficulties. (MB p. 7)

She insisted that the precision was worth the effort and expense. But she also noted that, on a related matter, "the engineer handling the negotiations broke down in a fit of sobbing. He did not want to give up the commission but despaired of ever being able to complete it in accordance with Ludwig's wishes" (p. 8).

Freedom of Religion

While defining "game" or a musical genre may seem like a pedantic exercise, the concept of "religion" can raise issues of real significance—such as, what practices are legally protected by the First Amendment to the US Constitution? It might be supposed that here we would require real precision.

In the 1890 case of *Davis v. Beason*, the US Supreme Court viewed religion in traditional theistic terms: "The term 'religion' has reference to one's views of his relations to his Creator, and to the obligations they impose of reverence for his being and character, and of obedience to his will." And it is natural to suppose that belief in some kind of Supreme Being would at least be a necessary condition for a practice to be religious.

But by the 1960s, the court acknowledged that a wide variety of practices deserved the title of "religion" without necessarily postulating the existence of a god. In *Torcaso v. Watkins*, in 1961, the court distinguished between: "those religions based on a belief in the existence of God as against those religions founded on different beliefs." It went on to list "religions in this country which do not teach what would generally be considered a belief in the existence of God ... Buddhism, Taoism, Ethical Culture, Secular Humanism and others."

The court was pressed to provide a fuller interpretation of the notion in a conscientious objection case, where the statute required belief in a "supreme being." In *United States v. Seeger*, the court considered "whether a given belief that is sincere and meaningful occupies a place in the life of its possessor parallel to that filled by the orthodox belief in God of one who clearly qualifies for the exemption." It held that "Where such beliefs have parallel positions in the lives of their respective holders we cannot say that one is 'in relation to a Supreme Being' and the other is not."

In essence, the court eventually went on to equate moral, ethical and religious principles, distinguishing them from considerations of policy, pragmatism, and expediency, and clarifying that they must be part of a consistent practice, which "precludes allowing every person to make his own standards on matters of conduct in which society as a whole has important interests" (*Wisconsin v. Yoder*, 1972).

Without naming Wittgenstein, the court has opted for a family resemblance understanding of the concept of "religion." Perhaps closer to American jurisprudential tradition is the Harvard philosopher-psychologist William James. In a favorite book of Wittgenstein's—*The Varieties of Religious Experience*, James set out a position in 1902 that Wittgenstein must have taken to heart:

> Most books on the philosophy of religion try to begin with a precise definition of what its essence consists of. Some of these would-be definitions may possibly come before us in later portions of this course, and I shall not be pedantic enough to enumerate any of them to you now. Meanwhile, the very fact that they are so many and so different from one another is enough to prove that the word "religion" cannot stand for any single principle or essence, but is rather a collective name. The theorizing mind always tends to the over-simplification of its materials. This is the root of all that absolutism and one-sided dogmatism by which both philosophy and religion have been infested. Let us not fall immediately into a one-sided view of our subject, but let us rather admit freely at the outset that we may very likely find no one essence, but many characters which may alternately be equally important in religion.

The US Supreme Court has, on this issue, avoided the kind of theorizing, over-simplification, and dogmatism that Wittgenstein and James opposed.

Analysis

In the *Tractatus*, Wittgenstein held that familiar facts could be broken down—analyzed—into facts at the most basic level—"atomic" facts. The notion of an "atom" comes directly from the ancient Greeks. The Greek word *atom* means *not-cut*. (Notice that in English, an appendectomy is where they *cut* out your appendix.) What the ancient Greek philosopher Democritus called an atom was a minute bit of matter that could not be broken down any further. Everything else was built up out of arrangements of these atoms. Wittgenstein had been interested in the search for logical (not physical) atoms–he was sure they existed, and he called them "objects."

It is an irony of history that during the Second World War, scientists in the United States figured out how to "split" the physical atom. To the ancient Greeks, that would have seemed to be a contradiction in terms. But it shows that what we might have supposed to be the most "basic" level turned out not to be basic after all. The atom was split into electrons, photons, protons and neutrons. And these, in turn, had been split into quarks. The search for "elementary" physical particles continues, but it is unclear if or where it will end.

In the *Investigations*, Wittgenstein took a much more pragmatic view of complexity. He no longer supposed that some things are inherently complex, or that there is some analysis that would reveal their true structure built up out of simple parts:

> But what are the simple constituent parts of which reality is composed?–What are the simple constituent parts of a chair?–The bits of wood of which it is made? Or the molecules, or the atoms?–"Simple" means: not composite. And here the point is: in what sense 'composite'? It makes no sense at all to speak absolutely of the 'simple parts of a chair'. (PI §47)

For an event planner, the chairs themselves would be the simple parts out of which arrangements could be made. For a woodworker, the legs and arms and seats would be the simple parts from which a chair could be built. And for a chemist, the cellulose fibers would be the simple parts out of which a piece of wood is composed.

You can't ask whether a particular object is composite or simple "*outside* a particular language game" (PI §47). The question only makes sense "if it is already established what kind of complexity–that is, what particular use of the word–is in question" (PI §47). The grammar of the language game tells us what counts or does not count as simple. So this is not a discovery so much as it is a stipulation. Wittgenstein now replied to a question about simplicity, in the abstract, apart from a purpose or context, by rejecting the question.

9-11 and the Twin Towers

On September 11, 2001, the twin towers of the World Trade Center in New York City were destroyed when they were hit by two Boeing 767 airliners piloted by suicide terrorists. In addition to the loss of thousands of lives, the material losses were in excess of $7 billion. The leaseholder for the World Trade Center sought insurance payment of this amount, but the insurance coverage was limited to $3.5 billion per insured "occurrence." The leaseholder claimed the destruction was two events, in which American Airlines Flight 11 hit the North Tower at 8:46 am local time, and then United Airlines Flight 175 hit the South Tower at 9:03 am local time. The insurance company argued the destruction constituted only one event, a "coordinated" attack in which a terrorist cell destroyed the World Trade Center. It turns out to make a huge difference whether it was one event or two.

Who was right? Wittgenstein's earlier account might have suggested that the leaseholder was right since the coordinated attack could be analyzed into two spatio-temporally separated crashes. But Wittgenstein's account in the *Investigations* suggests that it is important to determine the language game in which the question is being asked. For the purpose of discussing terrorist strategy, the coordinated attack seems to be a focus of attention. For the purpose of determining the impact on Lower Manhattan, there are two events to consider. There is no right answer in the abstract.

A federal jury ruled that there were two occurrences "for insurance purposes," siding with the leaseholder. Yet the finding by the U.S. District Court of Manhattan was that the leaseholder should collect $4.6 billion. Perhaps this was a sort of compromise to indicate the inherent indeterminacy of the issue. In any case, Wittgenstein showed why questions like this could not be answered without specifying the context and purpose for which the question is asked.

Meaning

In the Tractatus, Wittgenstein saw meaning as a matter of correspondence between language and the world. Language was about the world by being isomorphic with it. But even in the Tractatus Wittgenstein realized that there needed to be a way to indicate that something was meant to be a picture or a representation.

What does a word or phrase mean? Here is an answer offered by Humpty-Dumpty in Chapter VI of Lewis Carroll's "Through the Looking Glass":

> "[T]here are three hundred and sixty-four days when you might get un-birthday presents—"
> "Certainly," said Alice.
> "And only ONE for birthday presents, you know. There's glory for you!"
> "I don't know what you mean by 'glory'," Alice said.
> Humpty Dumpty smiled contemptuously. "Of course you don't—till I tell you. I meant 'there's a nice knock-down argument for you!'"
> "But 'glory' doesn't mean 'a nice knock-down argument'," Alice objected.
> "When I use a word," Humpty Dumpty said in rather a scornful tone, "it means just what I choose it to mean—neither more nor less."

"The question is," said Alice, "whether you CAN make words mean so many different things."

"The question is," said Humpty Dumpty, "which is to be master—that's all."

We might call this the "intention" theory of meaning. A word or phrase means whatever I intend it to mean. The above passage makes fun of the intention theory of meaning. If Alice had been thinking harder she would have asked Humpty Dumpty what he meant by "a nice knock-down argument," for this intention theory leads to an endless regress, and it can't be the whole story. But the moral here is that we can't make a word mean something just by intending it to.

Wittgenstein raised this issue in a similar way: "Can I say 'bububu' [this is a baby sound made by running your index finger up and down over your lips as you make a B sound] and mean 'If it doesn't rain I shall go for a walk'?" (PI, p. 22). You can certainly imagine that scenario or think that thought while you make that sound. But imagining it while you make the sound is not the same as meaning it by that sound. Wittgenstein continued: "It is only in a language that I can mean something by something. This shows clearly that the grammar of 'to mean' does not resemble that of the expression 'to imagine' and the like." In fact, when I mean or understand something, there may be all kinds of things going on in my mind at the time—I may even form pictures, but it is a mistake to suppose they constitute the meaning or understanding of the word or phrase.

What does constitute the meaning? In the *Tractatus*, Wittgenstein offered a theory of meaning. But in the *Investigations*, he wrote: "And we may not advance any kind of theory" (PI §109). He did bring up things designed to help loosen the hold misguided theories have on us. The Humpty-Dumpty story serves that purpose nicely. Wittgenstein wanted to remind us that we judge whether someone understands something not by how they feel about it inside, but by what they can do with it in practice—how the person can use it. Wittgenstein acknowledged both these aspects: the inner or subjective aspect of meaning–what he called grasping it "at a stroke" or "in a flash," and the outer or objective aspect of meaning–how it is used or applied (PI §138). Wittgenstein emphasized the outer aspect, while not entirely discounting the inner one because he did not offer an objective theory of meaning either. He put the point carefully: "For a large class of cases of the employment of the word 'meaning'–though not for all–this word can be explained in this way: the meaning of a word is its use in the language" (PI §43).

Flags and Mascots

In the United States, there has been a decades-long debate about the acceptability of displaying the Confederate battle flag. People whose ancestors fought in the Civil War on the side of the Confederacy (and their sympathizers) argue that the flag represents the values of historical commemoration, Southern or rural culture, and conservative politics. Yet, historically the flag has also been associated with the defense of slavery, racism, and White supremacy. Because of its negative associations, many people find the flag to be offensive, but its defenders have insisted that they do not mean to offend, but only to emphasize the flag's positive values.

To a certain extent, these are legal matters that involve the interpretation of free speech. The fact that these symbols are seen as "speech" confirms Wittgenstein's view of language games as not just language in the narrow sense. The relevant issue here is one of meaning–what does the flag mean or represent? Its advocates seem to be offering an intention theory of meaning–we don't intend any offense, therefore, the flag does not mean anything offensive. But is that an acceptable theory of meaning? According to Wittgenstein, meaning is something more than and apart from, what one has in mind.

On the other hand, opponents of the flag's display seem to be offering an interpretation theory of meaning—the flag is offensive because I take offense. Is that any better as a theory of meaning? When people complain about "political correctness," what bothers them is that too much weight is given to how something is perceived and to those who take offense.

This interpretation theory of meaning seems equally flawed. Several years ago, there were a few incidents in the United States in which some people were offended by the use of the word "niggardly." The word sounds like "nigger," which is almost universally agreed to be offensive, but in fact, it means "stingy" or "miserly," and has nothing to do with the racial slur. The fact that some people interpreted the word as a racial slur does not make it one.

It seems that meaning is not a matter of the intention of the user, and equally it is not a matter of the interpretation of the hearer. What is it then? If one thinks that meaning depends on use, then the issue is more complicated. It cannot be denied that the flag has been used for offensive purposes over many decades. Can it be "separated" from the offensive uses by contemporary attempts to use it in other ways? There has been a recent discussion of these issues in Europe surrounding the swastika. The symbol had a positive use for thousands of years before the Nazis appropriated it for evil use. Can that symbol ever be reclaimed?

Unfortunately, even though Wittgenstein highlighted the importance of use to meaning, he did not say much about how to assess use. We might ask: Whose use? Wittgenstein seemed to treat the users of the language as a monolithic group, without attending to the varieties of use, either at a time or over time. But this gives readers of the *Investigations* an opportunity to do some philosophy themselves. How might we deal with issues such as this, using the tools that Wittgenstein provided?

I have described the flag issue in some detail so that it can serve as a model for similar topics, such as the use of Native American images as mascots. While they have disappeared gradually at the high school level, they continue to be occasionally used at the college and professional levels. The professional baseball team in the city where I grew up, Cleveland, is called the "Indians," and the logo for the team is hard to look at. The professional football team that is close to where I live now, the Washington Redskins, has been strongly criticized for its name. The arguments over these matters have tended to follow the pattern of the flag arguments. Proponents of the name or logo emphasize the courage and honor of Native Americans; opponents see them as narrow caricatures of a legacy that was stolen from them. What would Wittgenstein say about these cases? How might they be discussed using Wittgenstein's tools?

Understanding and Rules

Do you understand addition? I hope any reader of this book does. Wittgenstein used this simple case, but the points he made are equally applicable to the question of understanding calculus or quantum physics. The question in this context raises the philosophical issue of what it takes to understand something. Generally, if you are asked whether you understand something, you can think about it for a moment and answer. You may well have a feeling of confidence, which leads you to answer affirmatively, or a feeling of confusion, which leads you to answer negatively. But, as with the discussion of meaning, a feeling of confidence is not the same thing as understanding. After all, you can feel confident and get something consistently wrong (we all know people like that), or feel confused and yet manage to get it consistently right. Understanding something is a matter of whether you can get it right. Wittgenstein compared our use of "understand" with "can," "is able to," and "to have 'mastered' a technique" (PI §150).

So, in essence, understanding addition is a matter of whether you have mastered the technique of adding. And that isn't something that we can necessarily take your word for. In general, whether we understand something is not a matter of our just saying so. What does it take to be able to add? What does it mean to get it right?

"Let us suppose that after some efforts on the teacher's part [the pupil] continues the series correctly, that is, as we do it. So now we can say that he has mastered the system" (PI §145). "As we do it." In writing this, Wittgenstein did not appeal to some transcendent numerical pattern to test our ability—it is tested by an appeal to how we do it. That might seem like a weak standard—couldn't "we" be doing it wrong?

That's a good question, and the answer depends on the case. But consider the case of understanding how to alphabetize a list. A student understands this process when she puts the list in alphabetical order—a, b, c, d....all the way to z. Yes, but couldn't that be wrong? That question really doesn't make sense. There is no "true" alphabetical order other than the one we use. Of course, we could have used a different order—but the order we use, the one we chose, couldn't be wrong. Wrong in light of what? There isn't anything further, any divinely ordained order, that it could be compared with.

But what about mathematics? Isn't there something like a divinely ordained order there? The case Wittgenstein discussed is "adding 2": 2, 4, 6, 8, 10....

> Let's suppose we have done exercises, and tested his understanding up to 1000.
>
> Then we get the pupil to continue ... beyond 1000—and he writes 1000, 1004, 1008, 1012.
>
> We say to him, "Look what you're doing!"—He doesn't understand. We say, "You should have added *two*: look how you began the series!"—He answers, "Yes, isn't it right? I thought that was how I *had* to do it."—Or suppose he pointed to the series and said, "But I did go on in the same way." (PI §185)

This is a hard scenario to wrap your head around. Clearly, the pupil has done it wrong. But (here's the philosophical problem), what makes it wrong? It is not simply a case where the pupil has misremembered, as when he says, "2, 4, 8, 12...." That directly contradicts the teacher's examples. We are supposed to imagine a case that goes beyond what has been explicitly taught. Even if the pupil was explicitly taught into the thousands, then we should imagine a scenario involving, say, 5-digit or 6-digit numbers. The point is that at some stage the student has to go on "in the same way," but without having had explicit guidance.

Yet, our feeling is that this pupil doesn't need explicit guidance because the initial guidance plus the nature of addition suffice to determine the next steps. It is as though the series of even numbers is laid out in heaven—visible to God, and to those who understand addition! How could the pupil go wrong in this way?

Let's try to put more flesh into this scenario than Wittgenstein did. For example, recall how our base-10 number system involves moving from 1-digit numbers to 2-digit numbers, and then to 3-digit numbers, and so on. Although we get the hang of those transitions, they are not obvious when you think about it, and they come up increasingly rarely. At a certain point in the training, you may have to just say, "that's how we do it—our number system is built to use only 10 different digits (i.e., it is base-10) and that is how we use it to count." Hardly anyone fails to get this way of using numbers. This is what Wittgenstein called sharing a "form of life."

Form of Life

Wittgenstein said little about forms of life, even though they played a large role in his thinking. So there is an inevitable amount of conjecture in how we fill out this notion. I would say that people share a form of life when they find it natural to go on in the same ways. The pupil who continues the series 2, 4, 6, 8, ... 1000, 1004, 1008, ... might be said not to find it natural to go on with the series in the way we do. In this sense, the person may (to that extent) not share our form of life.

Here are some illustrations that might seem more familiar. A child learns to look where you are pointing. A dog never does—a dog will only look at the end of your finger. A child finds it natural to attend to something you point at; a dog does not. To that extent, they do not share a form of life. A dog will generally learn to fetch; a cat will not. What dogs find natural to do, cats sometimes do not (and vice versa). What about humans? People generally learn to attend to and react to social cues from other people, but some people with autism do not naturally attend to or react to these cues. Perhaps we could say that they do not share a form of life in that respect.

In broad terms, I would say that sharing a form of life means being able to engage with one another and find common ground in ways that facilitate shared understanding and behavior. To engage in a language game together, it is essential to share a form of life. "The word 'language-game' is used here to emphasize the fact that the speaking of language is part of an activity, or a form of life" (PI §23). But we cannot identify or distinguish forms of life as we might identify or distinguish species of animals by inspecting them. "Form of life" is not a category so much as it is a tool for thinking about engagement with one another. Wittgenstein famously remarked: "If a lion could talk, we wouldn't be able to understand it" (PI, p. 235). Presumably, this is because we wouldn't share a form of life with the lion. Asserting that you share a form of life with another is essentially predicting that you will be able to engage productively over some range of activities.

The student mentioned above who incorrectly added 2 beyond 1000 got it wrong—not because there is a transcendent number line laid out in heaven, but because the pupil did not go on as we do. That is what makes us able to call such things right and wrong, according to Wittgenstein. A voice in the *Investigations* says: "So you are saying that human agreement decides what is true and what is false?" (PI §241). Of course, Wittgenstein did not want to say this, since it makes math sound arbitrary. He continued: "What is true or false is what human beings say; and it is in their language that human beings agree. This is agreement not in opinions, but rather in form of life." The objectivity of math comes not from a transcendent number line laid up in heaven, it comes from our sharing a form of life that allows for agreement when we do math. So, he went on to say that "odd as it may sound, agreement in judgements ... is required" (PI §242).

We can only sustain ideas of true and false, right and wrong, in a context in which there is general agreement about issues. And while such contexts of agreement usually also allow for common understandings of what constitutes reasons and justifications, if someone (like a 2-year-old) refuses to accept them and insists on asking "why?" then "Once I have exhausted the justifications, I have reached bedrock, and my spade is turned. Then I am inclined to say: 'This is simply what I do' " (PI §217). (I wish Wittgenstein had made his point here by saying, "This is what *we* do.")

Conversely, where we do not find a good deal of agreement in our reactions and judgments about a topic, we would not be able to sustain the notions of true and false, right and wrong. This implies that such notions are not appropriate in cases where there is significant ethical disagreement.

Communication and Community

Given Wittgenstein's emphasis on social context and community of agreement, it is interesting to examine what his own experiences were of communities in his life. He lived in many different settings. He grew up in a large close-knit family in turn-of-the-century Vienna, being schooled at home. In his mid-teens, he was sent to study at the Realschule in Linz for three years. And we have already mentioned his travels from there to Cambridge and, later, back to Cambridge.

When one talks of the "community," or what "we" would say, or how "we" would do it, it is natural to suppose that there is some single, well-defined group that is to be taken as the community, or who we are. But Wittgenstein's life did not seem to conform to that assumption. He lived in many communities, serially and sometimes alternately. But even if we focus on one of them, it was nearly always the case that he was "in" the community, but not "of" the community. He often lived as a stranger in a strange land. The community of agreement that plays a central role in his philosophical thinking seems largely lacking in his own experience of life.

The only setting that Wittgenstein seemed to consider a success was his life in Norway. He lived there, mostly in the village of Skjolden, for periods varying from a few weeks to several months at a time in 1913-14, 1921, 1931, 1936-37, and 1950, for a total of perhaps two years altogether. During the war, he had a small cabin built there for him so that he could easily return. (Though the cabin had been dismantled, its site can still be visited.) While living there for the longest stretch he wrote in his diary (October 16, 1937):

> Life here is on the one hand terrible for me, on the other hand it is something beautiful and friendly. In a sense I love my house and my food; I also feel a certain affection for the people here, who are always pleasant and friendly towards me. I get on well with them. I think it would be a bit sad for them if I left.

This is quite in contrast to his experiences with fellow soldiers in the war, with residents in the villages where he taught after the war, and with fellow academics in Cambridge. If Wittgenstein found community anywhere in his life, it was in Norway.

Thus, from the tenor of his philosophical remarks on the importance of agreement about how we do things, one would expect that here he would accept the practices and customs of the community, and be guided by the norms of his neighbors. Yet, based on research into specific interactions with others in the community of Skjolden, often the opposite occurred:

> Our oral sources...contribute an opposite shading to the portrait: that of a highly demanding and unusual figure. The aspect of conflict was...not absent. The fact that he wished to dictate the terms of social contact did occasionally lead to friction. We know of several examples where this is the case. The people in the village described him as "austere and dominating, meticulous and determined." On one occasion a local worker was asked to tar Wittgenstein's cottage [roof]. The man arrived five minutes late for the appointment at which they were to discuss the work. Wittgenstein turned out to be very offended by this, and exclaimed that anyone capable of such a thing ought to have his head chopped off. (WN, p. 30)

And:

> Among those Wittgenstein was well acquainted with in Skjolden was ... a figure known as "Old Galde".... Ola and Ludwig are reputed to have taken a walk together every Sunday. On a number of these walks Galde became irritated at Wittgenstein's tendency to swear, and one day said: "You, Wittgenstein, who are a fairly decent man, have to stop this cursing! It simply doesn't become you." Wittgenstein replied: "It's a way of getting rid of the devilry you have inside. You ought to swear more yourself."... The locals winced at what Wittgenstein dared say to him. It simply wasn't what they were used to. (WN, p. 26)

It is not that incidents like these are unfamiliar to students of Wittgenstein's life—they are all too familiar. But they illustrate that even in the rare context in which Wittgenstein felt himself to be at home, he still did not consider his fellow human beings or their behavior as any sort of standard or norm for himself. The fact that they had customs, such as not swearing, or being lax about appointments, had no relevance to him or his view of things.

A Norwegian acquaintance from much later in Wittgenstein's life said (WN, p. 173): "He could in many ways be authoritarian.... He had a remarkable ability to be independent. Other people are often dependent on their consciousness of the traditions they live in." But not Wittgenstein.

If he was not part of a real human community in Skjolden, then he didn't belong to any community during his lifetime. A student recalled: "Above all, his judgments were given with a directness and authority seldom met with, and with complete disregard of current intellectual, aesthetic, or moral fashions." So, how did the notion of community and agreement gain such a prominent place in Wittgenstein's philosophical remarks? How do we place his own authoritarian, anti-communal tendencies in relations to his remarks? What do we make of Wittgenstein's own unwillingness to defer to how "we" do things? These are not easy questions to answer.

Philosophy

Wittgenstein's views about the nature of philosophy did not change significantly over time, but he brought to bear some of the new tools that he had developed. At the time of the *Tractatus*, Wittgenstein warned about pseudo-propositions that looked like empirical propositions about the world but were not. In his later philosophy, he warned about the use of terms outside of the language games that were their homes.

In an introductory philosophy class, it is common for students to read Descartes' *Meditations*. In the first meditation, Descartes described a series of increasingly thoroughgoing ways in which we might be mistaken about the world around us—our perceptions might mislead us, we might be crazy and have delusions, we might be asleep and dreaming, or we might be fooled by an evil power (along the lines of the movie "The Matrix"). In light of these possibilities, it seems that we can't know anything for sure.

Descartes used a notion of knowledge that requires absolute certainty. And given these possibilities, it seems that we can't be certain about anything–so we don't really know. It is the job of the philosophy instructor to get the students to take this standard of knowledge seriously and to make them think that this is the real standard of knowledge.

The reason this is difficult is that we don't use this standard when we discuss knowledge. The concept of knowledge does have a place in many of our language games, but when it does, it comes with a set of (possibly vague and implicit) standards that allow us to judge when we do and when we do not know something. In the language games of the courtroom or the science lab the standards are much higher than in the language game of texting between friends. But in each of these contexts, we have an understanding of when we do and do not know something. And even if we are unsure, we have a sense of what it would take or how we could find out.

In the philosophy classroom, the implication of Descartes' scenarios is supposed to be that we could never know something (for sure), but that this is a kind of knowledge worth striving for. But Descartes and the philosophy instructor are using the word "know" with a sense that it does not have. There is no language game in which "know" has that grammar. Wittgenstein wrote, "When philosophers use a word–'knowledge', 'being', 'object', … –and try to grasp the essence of the thing, one must always ask oneself: is the word ever actually used in this way in the language in which it is at home?–What we do is to bring words back from their metaphysical to their everyday use" (PI §116).

Wittgenstein's thoughts about meaning illuminate the problem: If meaning is something internal–a feeling or an intention–then we could take a word and mean it as we like, in any sense and in any context, as long as we, the users, have the right internal something. The philosopher's question is meaningful as long as the words have the right feeling behind them. It is as though the words carry the meaning with them. Wittgenstein said: "I am told: 'You understand this expression, don't you? Well then–I'm using it with the meaning you're familiar with.' As if the meaning were an aura the word brings along with it and retains in every kind of use" (PI §117). But if the meaning of a word is its use, then it can't be separated from that use and be expected to retain its meaning.

This point is illustrated by Wittgenstein's famous example: "It is as if I were to say, 'You surely know what "It's 5 o'clock here" means; so you also know what "It's 5 o'clock on the sun" means. It means simply that it is just the same time there as it is here when it is 5 o'clock'" (PI §350). Well, a time of day is relative to the orientation of the Earth with respect to the Sun. So then to attempt to talk about the time of day on the sun is to attempt to use the notion without that relative orientation. The meaning of a word is relative to the language game in which it is used. To try to use the word outside that language game is to imagine that it carries its meaning with it independently of its home usage. This is what leads to philosophical confusions: "For philosophical problems arise when language goes on holiday" (PI §38). Language goes on holiday when it is set free from the work that it does in its home language game.

Another example of Wittgenstein's treatment of a philosophical problem might be the question whether our actions are ever free. In many ordinary contexts, we can discuss whether one has acted freely or not. We may not be acting freely if the wind blows at us uncontrollably, or we are threatened with death, or we are blackmailed. In these various contexts, we can discuss whether our action was free or constrained. But a philosopher tries to ask whether any of our actions are ever free. Or, whether we are truly free. Phrases like "truly free" and "really know," said with strong emphasis, are a warning that the discussion has transcended any ordinary language game. "The confusions which occupy us arise when language is, as it were, idling, not when it is doing work" (PI §132). Wittgenstein did not answer the question, but he did diagnose why it is misleading.

6. Wittgenstein's Applications

The discussions of freedom of religion, terrorist attacks on 9-11, and the Confederate flag introduced examples that Wittgenstein did not consider to illustrate how his thoughts about meaning could apply to familiar cases. But he did offer other examples. In each case, we can see how his tools and ways of thinking can be brought to bear on interesting topics.

The Inverted Spectrum

It is not uncommon to wonder whether other people see things the way you do. Of course, we know they often have different viewpoints on various issues, but in those cases, they can tell us so. Are there cases that go deeper? Could it be that the color I see when I look at a fire truck and call it "red" is really the color you see when you look at the sky and call it "blue"? When we both look at the fire truck, we both call it red. But couldn't my private experience—the reason I am calling the truck red—be different from your own experience, even though you too call it red? Maybe it's what I would call blue if I had it. How could we know?

The possibility of this sort of spectral inversion seems first to have been raised, rather briefly, in Plato's *Theaetetus* (153e-154a):

> Socrates: Let us follow what we stated a moment ago, and posit that there is nothing which is, in itself, one thing. According to this theory, black or white or any other color will turn out to have come into being through the impact of the eye upon the appropriate motion; and what we naturally call a particular color is neither that which impinges nor that which is impinged upon, but something which has come into being between the two, and which is private to the individual

percipient.–Or would you be prepared to insist that every color appears to a dog, or to any other animal, the same as it appears to you?

Theaetetus: No, I most certainly shouldn't.

Socrates: Well, and do you even feel sure that anything appears to another human being like it appears to you? Wouldn't you be much more disposed to hold that it doesn't appear the same even to yourself because you never remain like yourself?

Theaetetus: Yes, that seems to me nearer the truth than the other.

Wittgenstein was certainly familiar with this passage.

Here is the puzzle of the inverted spectrum–could your private color experience of the world be the inverse of mine? (Imagine the colors on a color wheel switched with the colors opposite them.) The puzzle is imagined to be unanswerable because there seems to be no way to test it–for all we know, my color experience of the world could be very different from yours. "The essential thing about private experience is really ... that nobody knows whether other people also have *this* or something else. The assumption would thus be possible–though unverifiable–that one section of mankind had one visual impression of red, and another section another" (PI §272).

Although I have put this passage in quotation marks because I was quoting it, Wittgenstein did not put it in quotation marks. If he had, it would have been a clear sign that it was a "voice" he was considering–but not necessarily his own view. Yet, in this case, he did *not* wish to endorse this passage. He was merely laying out a view that he thought was common but misguided.

While the inverted spectrum may be the form of the puzzle that is most commonly discussed, Wittgenstein had more to say about another version of the puzzle: whether your pain is the same as mine. What various versions of the puzzle have in common is that they all propose to consider an aspect of experience that we can't describe or characterize in any way–we can only *have* it. This is why it is called a "private" experience. Philosophers also sometimes call these private experiences "qualia."

Doctors and hospitals have tried to deal with this problem by introducing a "pain scale," where patients are asked to rate their pain from zero to 10, where zero means no pain and 10 means "the worst pain you can imagine." This scale is sometimes presented as a chart with cartoon faces with various increasingly pained expressions correlated with the numbers between zero and 10. But this in no way solves the problem described above. It only makes it more concrete—How do I know if "my" 6 is the same as "your" 6? When I call a pain "severe," do I mean the same as you when you call a pain "severe"? In general terms, this is what economists call the problem of "interpersonal comparison."

Wittgenstein found the notion of private experience that generates these puzzles problematic. The reason should be clear from what we found out already—it is an attempt to take the term "experience" from the language games in which it usually occurs, and use it beyond any language game. We do have a language game in which we can compare our experiences of pain—how much it hurts, when it hurts, where it hurts. This is the language game of the doctor's office and the hospital room. But the philosophical scenario specifically tries to transcend that language game. In fact, since it tries to focus on a notion of experience that transcends all description, it tries to transcend all language games. So the characterization of the scenario is confusing from the start.

Even if talk of private experience is not part of any language game, we might think that I could at least talk about it—to *myself*, so to speak. Couldn't I have a private language, maybe a diary, in which I record when I have certain pains (PI §258)? Wittgenstein rejected such a language, and this has come to be known as his private language argument. The basic idea is that language is a public phenomenon of following rules (of word usage). Language presupposes that words of the language are used properly, but the very notion of right and wrong usage itself requires a public check: "'following a rule' is a practice. And to *think* one is following a rule is not to follow a rule. And that's why it's not possible to follow a rule 'privately'; otherwise, thinking one was following a rule would be the same thing as following it" (PI §202).

This idea that following rules requires a public check is also connected with Wittgenstein's ideas about meaning. You might think that a private language would be legitimate because we can have right and wrong usage tied to following the meaning of the word. But meaning is not some internal thing–like an intention on my part. It is itself a matter of how it is used, and that requires a public context. In the inverted spectrum scenarios, we all use the word "red" in the same way–to apply to fire trucks. The scenario presupposes I could have some private meaning for red that is independent of how it is used. For Wittgenstein, however, "an 'inner process' stands in need of outward criteria" (PI §580).

Someone might respond: OK, maybe we can't talk about the scenario, especially if it transcends any language game, but that doesn't mean the scenario doesn't exist. Couldn't our color experience be inverted, even if we can't talk about it? (After all, recall the mystical realm in the Tractatus, which we couldn't talk about.)

Remember the earlier description of the scenario: "couldn't my private experience, that I am calling red, be different from your private experience, even though you too call it red? Maybe it's what I would call blue if I had it." What would it mean for me to have "had it" here? If I am calling it "blue," then that seems to prove that it's not what you had, since you called it "red." But the scenario requires that it be the very same experience.

If an experience were a thing, then we might have some handle on how it could exist and be the very same one independently of how it is described. For example, physical objects can be identified by where they are in space and time without worrying about their characteristics. Suppose I had a nickel in my pocket yesterday. Today, after my wife does the laundry, she finds a nickel in the dryer and claims it as her own. It is much shinier than the nickel I had yesterday. Even though we describe it differently (mine yesterday was dull, this one is shiny), still it might be the very same nickel I had yesterday. It would be the same one if it were spatio-temporally continuous with the one in my pocket yesterday. I'm not saying anyone actually tracked that nickel through the wash and dry cycles, but we know what it means to have the very same nickel even if it looks shinier now.

So, "I have a pain" looks like "I have a nickel." Grammatically they can both be named by nouns. Perhaps pains could be tracked and compared like nickels. The problem is that experiences are not like nickels. We don't have any handle on an experience to track whether it's the same one, apart from looking at how we describe it. Our language may mislead us into thinking that experiences are like things.

Wittgenstein's position is not only that we can't describe the inverted spectrum scenario because that would require a private language, but also that there is no such scenario–the very notion of private experience does not make sense.

Zombies

Let's say that a zombie is a human being that looks and acts just like us, but which doesn't have any conscious experiences. There's nothing that it is like to be a zombie. Since Wittgenstein rejected private experiences, did he mean to say that we are all really zombies? If so, *have* we no mental experiences, and we just go through the motions?

Wittgenstein imagined someone objecting: "'But you will surely admit that there is a difference between pain-behaviour with pain and pain-behaviour without pain.'" We can imagine that the zombie screams when you stab it (exhibiting "pain behavior") but doesn't really feel anything. The objection then is that there is a difference between zombies and humans. Wittgenstein replied: "Admit it? What greater difference could there be?" But then he imagined the objection: "'And yet you again and again reach the conclusion that the sensation itself is a Nothing.'" By rejecting the inverted spectrum scenario, Wittgenstein seemed to be saying that there is no "private experience" of color or pain that might differ from person to person, in ways that transcend any ability to describe the differences. Wittgenstein replied: "Not at all. It's not a Something, but not a Nothing either!"

This is one of my favorite lines in the *Investigations*. Experience is not a "Something"–i.e., it's not a "thing" like a nickel, yet Wittgenstein did not deny that we have experiences–i.e., it's not nothing. He continued: "The conclusion was only that a Nothing would render the same service as a Something about which nothing could be said." Wittgenstein objected to the notion of private experience that transcends any possible description–"about which nothing could be said." But he believed in experiences–the kind we all have and describe and compare. But they aren't "things." He concluded: "We've only rejected the grammar which tries to force itself on us here" (PI §304).

Wittgenstein did not think we are zombies–rather, he thought, as we all do, that we have experiences. But he didn't think that our experiences could be understood as *private* experiences, as experiences that transcend any possible description. Our experiences are just those that we describe and compare–an inverted spectrum that goes beyond describing is what is an illusion.

How Language Misleads Us

The grammar of our language treats both "pain" and "nickel" as nouns, and so tempts us to suppose that a pain and a nickel are both things, objects. But if "pain" is not the name of a thing, what is it? "Here is one possibility: words are connected with the primitive, natural expressions of sensation and used in their place. A child has hurt himself and cries; then adults talk to him and teach him exclamations and, later, sentences. They teach the child new pain behaviour. 'So you are saying that the word "pain" really means crying?'–On the contrary: the verbal expression of pain replaces crying, it does not describe it" (PI §244). It is interesting to note that we don't often say things like "I have a pain." But if we did, say in the doctor's office, Wittgenstein believed it would be much like saying "Ouch!" It is not a description of something or a statement that is true or false. It is an expression. It expresses pain, rather than describing it.

"The paradox disappears only if we make a radical break with the idea that language always functions in the same way, always serves the same purpose" (PI §304). In the *Tractatus*, Wittgenstein had initially believed that language always functions to say or describe–though he later added the function of showing. Later, in the *Investigations*, he acknowledged all kinds of functions (§23). Here we should consider that language expresses pain. And when he mentioned (in §304) "good and evil," I think he wanted us to consider that perhaps moral language expresses approval or disapproval, rather than describing or ascribing qualities of Goodness and Evil.

So, it takes a proper understanding of language to avoid some philosophical mistakes. While Wittgenstein valued our ordinary uses of language, where words do their work, he was also wary of its deceptions. And often its deceptions are built into the language, like ruts on a dirt road. Wittgenstein warned:

> People say again and again that philosophy doesn't really progress, that we are still occupied with the same philosophical problems as were the Greeks. But the people who say this don't understand why it has to be so. It is because our language has remained the same and keeps seducing us into asking the same questions. (CV, p. 15)

Where our language allows sensation words like "pain" to function in the same way as object words like "nickel," we have a rut. "For this purpose we shall again and again *emphasize* distinctions which our ordinary forms of language easily make us overlook" (PI §132).

Wittgenstein once told a friend: "I was thinking of using as a motto for my book a quotation from [Shakespeare's] *King Lear*: 'I'll teach you differences' " (CW, p. 157). We need to be sensitive to differences that language sometimes obscures.

The Fly Bottle

A fly-bottle is a container designed to trap a fly. (See the illustration on the front cover of this book.) It uses the fly's attraction to sweetened water to lure it into the bottle, and its attraction to light to keep it there.

The fly could get out the same way it got in, through the hole in the bottom, but it does not think to go out that way since that direction is darker than going upward. The fly's obsession with light will keep it from discovering the escape route and the solution to its problem. The fly is trapped by its own inclinations. Wittgenstein took our philosophical predicaments to be like the fly's predicament. Our philosophical puzzles come from being inclined to see things in misleading ways. It was not his task to formulate a philosophical theory, but to help us avoid these confusions that we bring on ourselves. "What is your aim in philosophy? −To show the fly the way out of the fly-bottle" (PI §309).

But how do you do that? Presumably, it is no easier than herding cats—which can't be done. We can't talk the fly out of the bottle since the fly already "knows" what it wants. For a long time, this famous line remained provocative but puzzling. Recently a manuscript was discovered in which Wittgenstein elaborated on this image:

> Cf. the fly catcher. If you want to let [the fly] out, you'd have to surround this by something dark. As long as there is light there, the fly can never do it.
>
> If I am puzzled philosophically, I immediately darken all

that which seems to me light, and try frantically to think of something entirely different. The point is, you can't get out as long as you are fascinated. The only thing to do is to go to an example where nothing fascinates me.

The fly is shown the way out by blocking the light that obsesses it so that only the downward, indirectly lighted direction remains attractive. This shows how much the process is a negative one, and also how much the process depends on knowing what happens to obsess the fly and how to redirect the fly's attention. Wittgenstein continued:

> First of all, it is not at all clear that this will help every fly.
> What happens to work with me doesn't work with him (Prof. Moore)–[what] works with me now, and may not work with me tomorrow.
> There are always new ways of looking at the matter.
> I constantly find new puzzles (I've thought about this for years, constantly ploughed these fields.) (WE, pp. 37-38)

When we are thinking about philosophical problems, we are often attracted to forming theories about them. This seems like "light" to us–the natural way to solve these issues. But Wittgenstein thought theories only exacerbate our problems since they take us further away from the natural home of our words. When he said he "darkens all that seems to me light," he meant that he tried to make us see the uselessness of philosophical theories, so that we will not be fascinated by them. Once we lose this fascination and recall the ordinary ways in which our words work, then the light of the downward direction will suffice as guidance. We must "look at an example, where nothing fascinates" us. We will go back to using words in ordinary ways, with our feet on solid ground.

But there is no one foolproof method, which works for all people or for all time. It depends on knowing what a person's temptations are. "The philosopher treats a question; like an illness" (PI §255).

"There is not a single philosophical method, though there are indeed methods, different therapies as it were" (PI §133).

Silence

What about those topics from the *Tractatus* about which we were to remain silent–ethics, religion, and the meaning of life? Recall that these things had to be shown rather than said.

The notion of showing does not retain an important place in Wittgenstein's later philosophy. But, on the other hand, he said rather little about these topics–almost nothing in the *Investigations*. So, in a way, he did remain silent about them. But the philosophical tools that he deployed did not require that silence. Certainly, there are ordinary language games that involve ethics or religion. In fact, religious ceremonies, such as prayer or worship, seem to offer perfect examples of language games. So Wittgenstein could have undertaken a survey of the language games of religion or ethics. This would have led to a "grammar" of those language games. He even mentioned: "Theology as grammar" (PI §373). But that's all he said about theology!

As little as Wittgenstein said about ethics and religion, we are left to conjecture how best to understand these matters in his terms. It might seem appropriate to treat religion as a language game. But a language game seems to require a set of roles, rules, and expectations. And different religions have different roles, rules, and expectations. So possibly different religions would be different language games. But even then, a whole religion seems too complex to be analyzed in this way. Perhaps it would make more sense to see various aspects of a religion–prayer, worship, confession–as language games themselves. Rather than ask, "what part of religion is a language game?" I think it makes more sense to ask, "how can the tools of language games best help us understand the various phenomena of religion?"

Similarly, some have thought that perhaps religion is a form of life. There is a sense in which what religious people find natural–say, thinking in terms of the creator and creature–scientifically-minded people do not find natural. So perhaps religion and science are two different forms of life. But in fact, some scientists are religious, and some religious believers are quite interested in science. So it is probably not productive to see these practices as wholly separate. Again, rather than ask whether religion or science are separate forms of life, I think it is more productive to ask how the tool of form of life can help us understand the practices of religion and science.

If we do decide to treat, say, two different ethical views as different language games, then this suggests a sort of separation between them that makes it unclear how they could communicate or engage. This might seem appropriate to pessimists who think that people with divergent viewpoints can only fight over their differences. But isn't it sometimes possible to engage productively, and even rationally, with people who have different views? We would then need to consider a higher-level language game of interaction between language games. We might call this the language game of dialogue between different points of view. To what extent can this lead to modification or reconciliation of language games? These questions can be addressed with Wittgenstein's tools, but also require some sociological experience to investigate.

As with the *Tractatus*, the fact that Wittgenstein did not say much about practical issues, such as ethics, does not mean he didn't care about them. In a letter from 1944 he wrote to a friend:

> [W]hat is the use of studying philosophy if all that it does for you is to enable you to talk with some plausibility about some abstruse questions of logic, etc., & if it does not improve your thinking about the important questions of everyday life.... You see, I know that it's difficult to think *well* about 'certainty', 'probability', 'perception', etc. But it is, if possible, still more difficult to think, or try to think, really honestly about your life and other people's lives. (MM, p. 35)

Just as Wittgenstein recommended silence at the end of the *Tractatus*, during his later career as a philosophy professor he regularly recommended that his students *not* be professors. He always preferred that they do other kinds of work, what he called "honest work" and "humanly valuable" occupations, perhaps bringing their philosophical skills to bear in those realms. He did not regard professional philosophy as honest work.

> He had an abhorrence of academic life in general and of the life of a professional philosopher in particular. He believed that a normal human being could not be a university teacher and also an honest and serious person. (MM, p. 28)

Nevertheless, several of his students became philosophy professors after all.

Could a Machine Think?

In 1939, Wittgenstein devoted his classes to topics in the foundations of mathematics. Among the people attending the classes was Alan Turing, who had recently earned his Ph.D. in mathematics, and was now a fellow of King's College at Cambridge. Turing soon went on to work for British Intelligence during World War II, assigned to break the German secret Enigma code. To accomplish this task, he essentially invented the computer, which could work through huge numbers of possibilities much faster than humans could. (This was the subject of the 2014 movie "The Imitation Game.") Turing and his co-workers later became interested in programming a computer to play chess, since this also involved working through possibilities rapidly. While breaking codes and playing chess are fairly narrowly defined tasks, they depend on abilities that are common to many tasks that require intelligence. Could computers, programmed to perform these narrowly defined tasks, eventually be able to perform a wider range of tasks? Could they eventually even think?

Recall the way Socrates would respond to difficult questions of this sort. He would reframe the question to focus on the controversial concept: "What do you mean by 'think'?" Turing set out to address this philosophical question in his seminal 1950 paper, "Computing Machinery and Intelligence": "The original question 'Can machines think?' I believe to be too meaningless to deserve discussion" (CMI, p. 449), so he designed a test. Turing was also afraid that people would automatically feel that computers could not think and that this was a sort of prejudice. Just as men through history had been prejudiced against people of other races or against women, so too we may also be biased against silicon-based entities that are not made of the same carbon-based stuff as we are. Therefore, he wanted to find a test that would prevent these kinds of prejudices from coming into play.

Turing proposed that we test an entity's ability to think according to its ability to answer a wide range of questions plausibly. If we take an adult human of normal intelligence, who obviously can think, and a computer, and we are allowed to submit questions digitally, the computer could be said to "think" if we are unable to tell which is the computer and which is the human after comparing their digitally conveyed answers over some period. This came to be known as the "Turing Test," though he called it the "imitation game." Of course, computers in 1950 were far from being able to pass the test. But Turing predicted "that in about fifty years' time it will be possible to program computers, with a storage capacity of about 10^9, to make them play the imitation game so well that an average interrogator will not have more than 70 per cent chance of making the right identification after five minutes of questioning" (CMI, p. 449). Clearly, Turing was making some rather arbitrary (yet educated) guesses here, but his main point is clear–computers would be able to pass the test in the foreseeable future. And, more importantly, there is nothing about a computer that inherently prevents it from being able to pass the test. Much of his paper is devoted to countering the numerous possible objections.

Wittgenstein's approach to this issue was typical—conversational, brief, and inconclusive. He did not use quotation marks to indicate different voices, but dashes:

> Could a machine think?—Could it be in pain?—Well, is the human body to be called such a machine? Surely it comes as close as possible to being such a machine.
>
> But surely a machine cannot think!—Is that an empirical statement? No. We say only of a human being and what is like one that it thinks. We also say it of dolls and perhaps even ghosts. Regard the word "to think" as an instrument! (PI §359-360)

In an earlier passage he had written: "It amounts to this: that only of a living human being and what resembles (behaves like) a living human being can one say: it has sensations; it sees; is blind; hears; is deaf; is conscious or unconscious" (PI §281).

One of these voices seems to express just the sort of prejudice that Turing feared—that only human beings could think. And it was certainly true that in the mid-20th century, and even now, we don't speak of machines thinking in our ordinary language games. So, on a use-theory of meaning machines don't and couldn't think.

But the voice is not actually that strict, for it allows us to say this of humans and "what is like one" or "what resembles (behaves like)" one. Could a machine be "like" a human in relevant respects—especially in respect to behavior? Well, this is exactly the point that Turing tried to make—that machines could behave like humans. Turing saw this as an empirical issue whether and when it might be accomplished. But a voice asks whether this is an empirical issue, and answers that it is not.

Wittgenstein then acknowledged that we do extend the use of "thinking" to things beyond humans—dolls and ghosts, for instance—at least in a manner of speaking. And, on the other hand, he reminded us that a human being could be thought of as a machine. This, in fact, is crucial to the research program of artificial intelligence. Human abilities can be represented, and thus replicated, in machine-like ways.

Turing's prediction that machines might well pass the test "in fifty years' time" did not turn out to be true. There have been Turing Test competitions for decades now, and no computer has come close to passing the test. Automated customer service calls are probably familiar to most readers of this book. They are notoriously frustrating. Online "chatterbots" are specifically designed to engage in conversations that approximate the Turing Test. The 2013 film "Her" starred a phone operating system that clearly would pass the Turing Test (if it were real).

But in 1997, IBM's computer Deep Blue won a chess match against the reigning (human) World Champion Garry Kasparov. IBM's computer Watson beat two human champions in a two-day Jeopardy match in 2011. (Watson had 4 terabytes of memory—4 x 10^{12}.) And Google has now designed a successful self-driving car.

While we should discount his overly optimistic expectation, Turing concluded: "I believe that at the end of the century the use of words and general educated opinion will have altered so much that one will be able to speak of machines thinking without expecting to be contradicted" (CMI, p. 449). Wittgenstein would acknowledge that our language games can and do evolve over time. And this is certainly one way that they could change. Wittgenstein's proposal: "Regard the word 'to think' as an instrument!" supports the notion that our concepts are dynamic tools for understanding the world, not passive labels to be attached once and for all.

In the later remarks attached to the *Investigations*, Wittgenstein had an extended discussion of "seeing as." His famous illustration is the duck-rabbit figure, which can be seen *as* a duck or *as* a rabbit (PI, p. 204). (See illustration.)

What do you see? A duck or a rabbit?

His proposal that we see the concept of "thinking" as an instrument suggests that we can opt to see a machine as thinking, for certain purposes. So the issue is not whether we can discern "thinking" in the machine, but whether it is helpful to treat the machine as thinking. In another passage, Wittgenstein wrote: "My attitude towards him is an attitude towards a soul. I am not of the *opinion* that he has a soul" (PI, p. 187). Rather than form an opinion about whether something thinks or has a soul, one takes up an attitude towards it as thinking or having a soul. This might express itself in how we treat it or interact with it. This is indicative of the sort of pragmatic approach that is taken by researchers in artificial intelligence.

The Ladder

Wittgenstein presented the propositions of the *Tractatus* as a ladder that would bring the reader to a new place. From this new place, the reader would appreciate the limits of language. In the *Investigations*, Wittgenstein was concerned that the reader had been disoriented, and his task was to bring the reader back to Earth–back to the solid ground of ordinary language. In a way, that is where the reader already is, but the reader may have thought that somewhere else would be better–somewhere founded on a philosophical theory: "I might say: if the place I want to get to could only be reached by way of a ladder, I would give up trying to get there. For the place I really have to get to is a place I must already be at now. Anything that I might reach by climbing a ladder does not interest me [any more]" (CV, p. 7).

This raises the question of whether or how an enlightened philosopher is any better off than a person who never gave a thought to philosophy. One might think that on Wittgenstein's view, there is no difference.

For comparison, consider the character Platon from Tolstoy's *War and Peace*. The protagonist, Pierre, meets Platon in a prisoner of war camp. Platon is the archetypal good Russian peasant and soldier:

> To all the other prisoners Platon Karataev seemed a most ordinary soldier. They called him "little falcon" or "Platosha," chaffed him good-naturedly, and sent him on errands. But to Pierre he always remained what he had seemed that first night: an unfathomable, rounded, eternal personification of the spirit of simplicity and truth. Platon Karataev knew nothing by heart except his prayers. When he began to speak he seemed not to know how he would conclude.
>
> Sometimes Pierre, struck by the meaning of his words, would ask him to repeat them, but Platon could never recall what he had said a moment before, just as he never could repeat to Pierre the words of his favorite song: "native" and "birch tree" and "my heart is sick" occurred in it, but when spoken and not sung, no meaning could be got out of it. He did not, and could not, understand the meaning of words apart from their context. Every word and action of his was

the manifestation of an activity unknown to him, which was his life. But his life, as he regarded it, had no meaning as a separate thing. It had meaning only as part of a whole of which he was always conscious. His words and actions flowed from him as evenly, inevitably, and spontaneously as fragrance exhales from a flower. He could not understand the value or significance of any word or deed taken separately. (Book 1, Part 4, Chapter 13)

Platon's conversation embodies the conception of language that Wittgenstein once offered to a friend as summarizing a good deal of his philosophy: "An expression has meaning only in the stream of life" (MM, p. 75). A person such as this could not get into philosophical confusions. But would we want to be Platon, incapable of philosophical confusion, or even philosophical reflection?

Wittgenstein is sometimes called an "anti-philosopher." You can see why he would get that label if his goal were to (get us to) become like Platon. This criticism might be reinforced with the quotation from Wittgenstein's notebook: "Philosophy is a tool which is useful only against philosophers and against the philosopher in us." But is the philosopher in us just an illness?

The comparison of philosophical puzzlement to an illness (PI §255) raises the parallel question of whether or how a person cured of an illness is better off than a person who never contracted it. A cured person may have two advantages—she may have acquired an immunity to the illness or learned how to cure the illness, which can then be an advantage to others as well.

But, despite his comparison, I don't think Wittgenstein saw philosophical problems as simply illnesses. For he also regarded the temptations that get us into philosophical problems as natural—either built into the language or into our psyche. Could a natural condition really be considered an illness?

Someone who doesn't even encounter philosophical problems is not fully aware or fully reflective. While the cure for philosophical temptation is to appreciate the ordinary language games where our words have their homes, this appreciation isn't complete unless it is accompanied by awareness of its challenges and its alternatives. While there is something to admire in Platon, there is also something missing in him.

When Wittgenstein compared himself to a tour guide, he implied that philosophical puzzlement is like being lost: "A philosophical problem has the form: 'I don't know my way about' " (PI §123). Doesn't a lost person need to get somewhere else, even if not by a ladder? Not necessarily, for not knowing your "way about" does not mean you are in the wrong place—just that you are disoriented. Someone who was disoriented and now is oriented may have the advantage of knowing the lay of the land better. How is a tour guide better than a local? Imagine Platon offering these directions to a person who is lost: "Go down this road and then turn left where that old trailer used to be."

Wittgenstein's contemporary, T. S. Eliot, captured the notion of reorientation in the poem "Little Gidding" from his *Four Quartets* series (1942):

> We shall not cease from exploration
> And the end of all our exploring
> Will be to arrive where we started
> And know the place for the first time.

There is a kind of knowledge of place that comes from having been displaced. It is a critical awareness in place of a naïve unawareness.

7. The End

Wittgenstein retired from teaching in 1947 to focus on finishing his book, and to avoid the distractions of teaching. He spent much of the time in retirement in Ireland—first in Dublin and then on the western coast. But he became ill and eventually lived with friends in Oxford and finally in Cambridge.

Through his life, Wittgenstein lived in many places. I have called him an "exile" (WE, p. 48), though his exile was as much a cultural as it was a geographical one. His travels certainly suited him to be the tour guide that he had imagined as a metaphor for the philosopher. But these journeys were often motivated by the desire to escape some situation and to find solitude to do his work. I don't think that either in his geographical travels or in the journeys of his life, Wittgenstein ever found the place he searched for, or the satisfaction he sought from the place where he was. This is indicated by his continual moves and by his inability to finish his book. In the *Investigations*, he said, "The real discovery is the one that enables me to break off philosophizing when I want to.–The one that gives philosophy peace..." (PI §133). But later, when discussing with a friend this idea that one can reach a resting place and stop doing philosophy, Wittgenstein remarked: "That's a lie! I *can't*" (CW, p. 219). He never felt he made that "real discovery."

One evening shortly before his death, Wittgenstein recalled for a friend the inscription Bach added on the title page of his *Little Organ Book*: "To the glory of the most high God, and that my neighbor may be benefited thereby." Pointing to his own pile of manuscripts he said, "That is what I would have liked to have been able to say about my own work." Yet, his friend and student, Elizabeth Anscombe, recalled: "I once heard someone ask Wittgenstein what it all came to, what was so to speak the upshot, of the philosophy he was teaching in the 1940's. He did not answer."

There is no culmination of Wittgenstein's work—no final insight.

What there is, and what remains his real contribution, is a set of tools for thinking about various topics, and many examples of how he grappled with those issues.

A Wonderful Life

Wittgenstein died on April 29, 1951. He had suffered from cancer for a few years, finally taking hormone and x-ray treatments. But he gave them up in February of that year, and his physician Dr. Edward Bevan and his wife invited him to stay with them during his final months. Many years later, Bevan wrote: "I have never met anyone who made a greater impression upon me, and I came to respect and love him. He was a great and a good man, above all ... honest, humble, unafraid and grateful: and I don't think he was unhappy at the end."

As his condition worsened on April 28, Wittgenstein was informed that his friends would be coming the next day. His last words said (in English) to Mrs. Bevan before losing consciousness were (MM, p. 81): "Tell them I've had a wonderful life!"

Was this an accurate description of Wittgenstein's life? Did he mean to say something true, or something consoling for his friends? What did he mean by "wonderful?" (How) can we understand this? Mrs. Bevan offered no interpretation. Norman Malcolm, one of his friends, who, however, was not in England at the time, first published these words in 1958. He found them to be a mystery:

> When I think of his profound pessimism, the intensity of his mental and moral suffering, the relentless way in which he drove his intellect, his need for love together with the harshness that repelled love, I am inclined to believe that his life was fiercely unhappy. Yet at the end he himself exclaimed that it had been 'wonderful'! To me this seems a mysterious and strangely moving utterance. (MM, p. 81)

Then, in a revised edition in 1984 he decided (p. 84) that, though Wittgenstein's life seemed unhappy, he must have derived considerable satisfaction from his work and friendships.

In 1958, Malcolm interpreted "wonderful" as synonymous with "enjoyable." By 1984, however, he saw it as synonymous with "worthwhile." Another model for Wittgenstein's sense of the word could be Frank Capra's 1946 film, "It's a Wonderful Life." Indeed, it is hard to imagine Wittgenstein, a great fan of popular American films, making this statement without being aware of its similarity to the title of this film. Yet, it is hard to see what this similarity might have been. None of these interpretations seems satisfying.

Another scholar has proposed to interpret "wonderful" literally as "full of wonder" (WW, p. 510). Though this stretches its colloquial use in English, Webster's 2nd Edition does offer "adapted to excite wonder." It is clear that the capacity to wonder was important for Wittgenstein. In 1929, in his "Lecture on Ethics," he offered "wonder at the existence of the world" (PO, p. 41) as an illustration of what had intrinsic value for him. And he feared that this capacity for wonder was endangered by modern conceptions of science and progress: "Man has to awaken to wonder... Science is a way of sending him to sleep again" (CV, p. 5). The progress of modern science, perhaps, "always looks much greater than it really is."

Wittgenstein strove to have a life of wonder, and this construal of his dying words would, in a sense, crown that life. If we can achieve a view of the world unconstrained by theories and untainted by a misunderstanding of language, we may find ourselves, as Wittgenstein once put it, "walking on a mountain of wonders" (WT, p. 186).

Sources

AL – Stanley Cavell, "The Availability of Wittgenstein's Later Philosophy," in *Must We Mean What We Say?* Cambridge, 1976.

AW – Anthony Kenny, "Aquinas and Wittgenstein," *Downside Review*, v. 77, 1959.

BW – Ludwig Hänsel, *Begegnungen mit Wittgenstein: Ludwig Hänsels Tagebücher* 1918/1919 und 1921/1922, edited by Ilse Somavilla, Haymond, 2012.

CMI – Alan Turing, "Computing Machinery and Intelligence," in *The Essential Turing*, edited by B. Jack Copeland, Oxford, 2004.

CV – Ludwig Wittgenstein, *Culture and Value*, translated by Peter Winch, Blackwell, 1980.

CW – M. O'C. Drury, "Conversations with Wittgenstein," in *Recollections of Wittgenstein*, edited by Rush Rhees, Oxford, 1984.

DG – Ray Monk, *Ludwig Wittgenstein: The Duty of Genius*, Free Press, 1990.

EU – Plato, "Euthyphro," in *Five Dialogues*, 2nd Edition, Hackett, 2002.

GJ – D.A.T. Gasking and A.C. Jackson, "Ludwig Wittgenstein," in *Portraits of Wittgenstein*, Volume 4, edited by F.A. Flowers III, Thoemmes, 1999.

GT – Ludwig Wittgenstein, *Geheime Tagebücher*, edited by Wilhelm Baum, Turia & Kant, 1991.

IS – Daniel Dennett, *The Intentional Stance*, MIT, 1987.

LF – Ludwig Wittgenstein, "Letters to Ludwig von Ficker," in

Wittgenstein: Sources and Perspectives, edited by C.G. Luckhardt, Cornell, 1979.

LM – J. E. Littlewood, *Littlewood's Miscellany*, edited by Bela Bellobas, Cambridge, Revised edition, 1986.

LO – Ludwig Wittgenstein, *Letters to C.K. Ogden*, edited by G.H. von Wright, Blackwell, 1973.

LP1 – Leiter Reports: A Philosophy Blog, "So who is the most important philosopher of the past 200 years?" Poll results posted March 11, 2009: http://leiterreports.typepad.com/blog/2009/03/so-who-is-the-most-important-philosopher-of-the-past-200-years.html

LP2 – Leiter Reports: A Philosophy Blog, "The 20 'Most Important' Philosophers of the Modern Era," Poll results posted May 4, 2009: http://leiterreports.typepad.com/blog/2009/05/the-20-most-important-philosophers-of-the-modern-era.html

LP3 – Leiter Reports: A Philosophy Blog, "The 20 'Most Important' Philosophers of All Time," Poll results posted May 18, 2009: http://leiterreports.typepad.com/blog/2009/05/the-20-most-important-philosophers-of-all-time.html

MB – Hermine Wittgenstein, "My Brother Ludwig," in *Recollections of Wittgenstein*, edited by Rush Rhees, Oxford, 1984.

MM – Norman Malcolm, *Ludwig Wittgenstein: A Memoir*, Oxford, 2nd Edition, 1984.

MPD – Bertrand Russell, *My Philosophical Development*, Routledge, 1995.

NB – Ludwig Wittgenstein, *Notebooks: 1914-1916*, translated by G.E.M. Anscombe, Blackwell, 1979.

PE – Paul Engelmann, *Letters from Ludwig Wittgenstein with a Memoir*, edited by B.F. McGuinness, Blackwell, 1967.

PI – Ludwig Wittgenstein, *Philosophical Investigations*, Revised 4th edition, translated by G.E.M. Anscombe, P.M.S. Hacker and Joachim Schulte, Wiley-Blackwell, 2009.

PLA – Bertrand Russell, *The Philosophy of Logical Atomism*, edited by David Pears, Open Court, 1985.

PO – Ludwig Wittgenstein, *Philosophical Occasions: 1912-1951*, edited by James C. Klagge and Alfred Nordmann, Hackett, 1993.

PPO – Ludwig Wittgenstein, *Public and Private Occasions*, edited by James C. Klagge and Alfred Nordmann, Rowman & Littlefield, 2003.

PU – J.L. Austin, "Performative Utterances," in *Philosophical Papers*, Third Edition, Oxford, 1979.

SG – Bernard Suits, *The Grasshopper: Games, Life and Utopia*, Broadview, 2005.

TLP – Ludwig Wittgenstein, *Tractatus Logico-Philosophicus*, translated by David Pears and B.F. McGuinness, Routledge Kegan Paul, 1963.

VC – Friedrich Waismann, *Wittgenstein and the Vienna Circle: Conversations Recorded by Friedrich Waismann*, edited by Brian McGuinness, Blackwell, 1979.

VW – Ludwig Wittgenstein and Friedrich Waismann, *The Voices of Wittgenstein: The Vienna Circle*, edited by Gordon Baker, Routledge, 2003.

WA – Ludwig Wittgenstein, *Wiener Ausgabe, Band. 2*, edited by Michael Nedo, Springer, 1994.

WE – James C. Klagge, *Wittgenstein in Exile*, MIT, 2011.

WL – Brian McGuinness, *Wittgenstein: A Life, Young Ludwig (1889-1921)*, Blackwell, 1988.

WN – Knut Amas and Rolf Larsen, "Ludwig Wittgenstein in Norway: 1913-1950," in *Wittgenstein in Norway*, edited by K. Johannessen and K. Amas, Solum Forlag, 1994.

WP – David Stern, *Wittgenstein's Philosophical Investigations*, Cambridge, 2004.

WT – G.E.M. Anscombe, "Wittgenstein's 'Two Cuts' in the History of Philosophy," in *From Plato to Wittgenstein: Essays by G.E.M. Anscombe*, eds., M. Geach and L. Gormally, Imprint Academic, 2011.

WW – Peter John, "Wittgenstein's Wonderful Life," *Journal of the History of Ideas*, v. 49, 1988.

Suggested Reading

I n this book, I have focused almost exclusively on Wittgenstein's two great works, the *Tractatus* and the *Investigations*. Many of his other writings have also been published since his death. All of his 20,000 pages of notebooks and drafts are available on CD-ROM, and much of that is freely available on-line at Wittgenstein Source (http://www.wittgensteinsource.org). Some 25 volumes of Wittgenstein's work have been published in (paper) book form as well. But these two books should be the starting place for anyone wanting to study Wittgenstein. Near the end of his life, he wrote extensive notes about knowledge and certainty. These were collected and published together as *On Certainty* (OC). These notes are mostly compatible with the ideas of the *Investigations*, but also develop some ideas in new directions. The last remark collected in *On Certainty* was written two days before his death. If you want to read more by Wittgenstein, it would make sense to read this compilation next.

Wittgenstein led a fascinating life. I have mentioned some aspects of it, but only when they impacted his philosophy in an interesting way. Anyone wanting to know more about his life should read Ray Monk's biography, *Ludwig Wittgenstein: The Duty of Genius* (DG). This book also gives helpful explanations of Wittgenstein's philosophical views along the way. In general, I think that Wittgenstein's work is best understood in the context of his life. But since his work was such an integral part of his life, it is futile to try to understand his life without reading his work.

Over the years, Wittgenstein had many friends and acquaintances, and several of them wrote about their relationship with him. They give important insights into his motivations and views on a wide range of topics. I have quoted from two of these memoirs: Paul Engelmann (PE) knew Wittgenstein especially around the time of the *Tractatus*, and Norman Malcolm (MM) knew

Wittgenstein later in his life, around the time he was working on the *Investigations*. They both also include the letters that Wittgenstein wrote to those authors, which make for good reading. They constitute good starting places for a personal perspective on Wittgenstein.

Literally hundreds, perhaps thousands of books have been written by scholars offering to explain and interpret Wittgenstein's philosophy. This book adds one to that number. Something that strikes me, however, is how emphatic Wittgenstein was that people would *not* understand his philosophy! What should we make of this? My attempt to figure this out led to *Wittgenstein in Exile*, a book that I wrote and published a few years ago (WE). I use information about Wittgenstein's life and his views about himself to help make sense of why his philosophy might be so hard to understand. A reader who has enjoyed reading this book might read that one as well to find where I go from here.

Readers who are interested in following Wittgenstein's approach to philosophy into the present might consider the approach that Daniel Dennett has taken toward research on the mind. Dennett, like Wittgenstein, sees our concepts as instruments, and he distinguishes between the *intentional stance* and the *mechanistic stance* toward entities (IS). Dennett has argued against some of Wittgenstein's views as they are traditionally presented, but I think my understanding of Wittgenstein's views makes them more amenable to Dennett's work in philosophy and cognitive science.

As I mentioned in the Preface to this book, Wittgenstein has influenced contemporary Western culture in many ways *outside* of philosophy. The influences are so diverse that I can't list examples of each, but for just one example the reader might like to listen to compositions by Steve Reich. *Music for 18 Musicians*, for instance, can be thought of as a meditation on musical language games. His composition, "Explanations Come to an End Somewhere," on the disc, *You Are (Variations)*, is a musical setting for Wittgenstein's oft-used line: "Explanations come to an end somewhere" (PI §1). In his "Composer's Notes" for the composition "Proverb" Reich concludes:

The short text, "How small a thought it takes to fill a whole life!" comes from a collection of Wittgenstein's writing entitled *Culture and Value*. Much of Wittgenstein's work is 'proverbial' in tone and in its brevity. This particular text was written in 1946. In the same paragraph from which it was taken Wittgenstein continues, "If you want to go down deep you do not need to travel far." (CV, p. 50)

The reader, and now listener, might wish to reflect on how Wittgenstein came back to the same few issues over and over, and on whether he did "travel far" or not.

About the Author

James C. Klagge is Professor of Philosophy at Virginia Tech, where he has taught for over 30 years. He has written, edited or co-edited four books on Wittgenstein, including *Wittgenstein in Exile* (2011), *Ludwig Wittgenstein: Public and Private Occasions*(2003), and *Wittgenstein: Biography and Philosophy* (2001). Klagge has a special interest in Wittgenstein's experiences as a teacher, and how they influenced his thought and writing.

Afterword

Thank you for reading *Simply Wittgenstein*!

If you enjoyed reading it, we would be grateful if you could help others discover and enjoy it too.

Please review it with your favorite book provider such as Amazon, BN, Kobo, iBooks or Goodreads, among others.

Again, thank you for your support and we look forward to offering you more great reads.

Printed in Great Britain
by Amazon

58513750R00078